JAMES TAYLOR

SIGNATURE SOUNDS AND TABS

Contents

Introduction

James Taylor, with his distinctive voice and masterful guitar prowess, has serenaded generations with songs that echo sentiments of love, longing, joy, and introspection. His music transcends eras, offering solace and comfort, like an old friend sitting across the room with a guitar, strumming tales of times gone by. This bond between Taylor and his listeners is a testament to the timelessness of his artistry.

"James Taylor: Signature Sounds and Tabs" endeavors to bridge the gap between the auditory magic of Taylor's classics and the tangible art of guitar playing. This book isn't just a collection of tablatures—it's an invitation to delve deeper into the musical world of one of America's most cherished songwriters. Whether you're a novice, hoping to strum along to "Carolina In My Mind," or an adept player aiming to capture the nuance of "Fire and Rain," this compilation serves as your guide.

Drawing inspiration from iconic tracks spanning Taylor's illustrious career, this collection is both a celebration of his musical genius and a tool for aspiring guitarists to tap into the soul of his songs. By breaking down each melody, chord progression, and intricate fingerstyle pattern, we've endeavored to provide a pathway for you to not just play but feel each song.

As you turn the pages and traverse through these tabs, may you find the same warmth, passion, and familiarity that millions have discovered in James Taylor's music. Let every pluck, every chord, and every strum resonate with the heart and spirit of this legendary artist. Welcome to "James Taylor: Signature Sounds and Tabs."

Carolina In My Mind

James Taylor

Tuning: E A D G B E

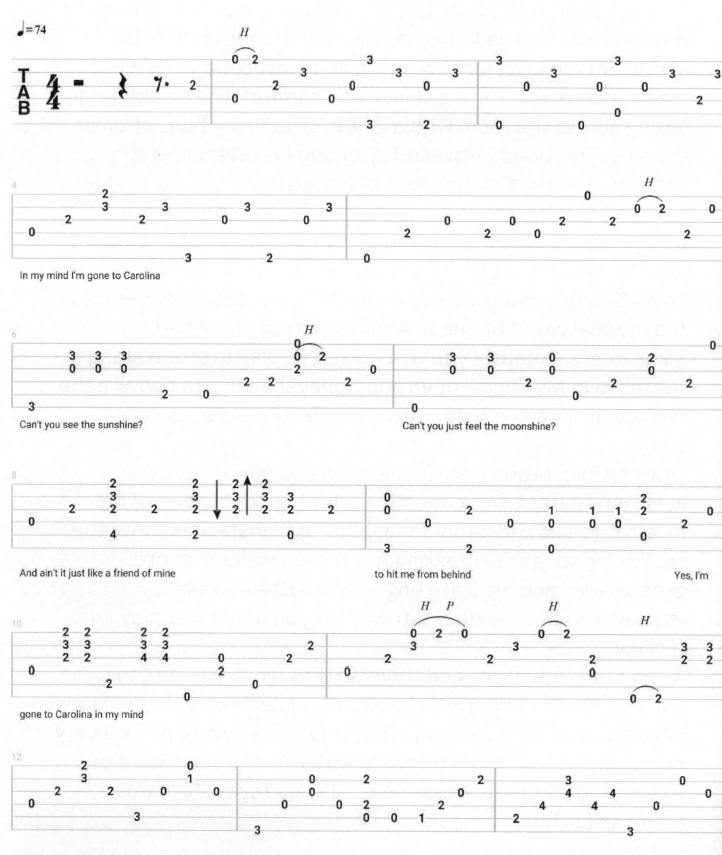

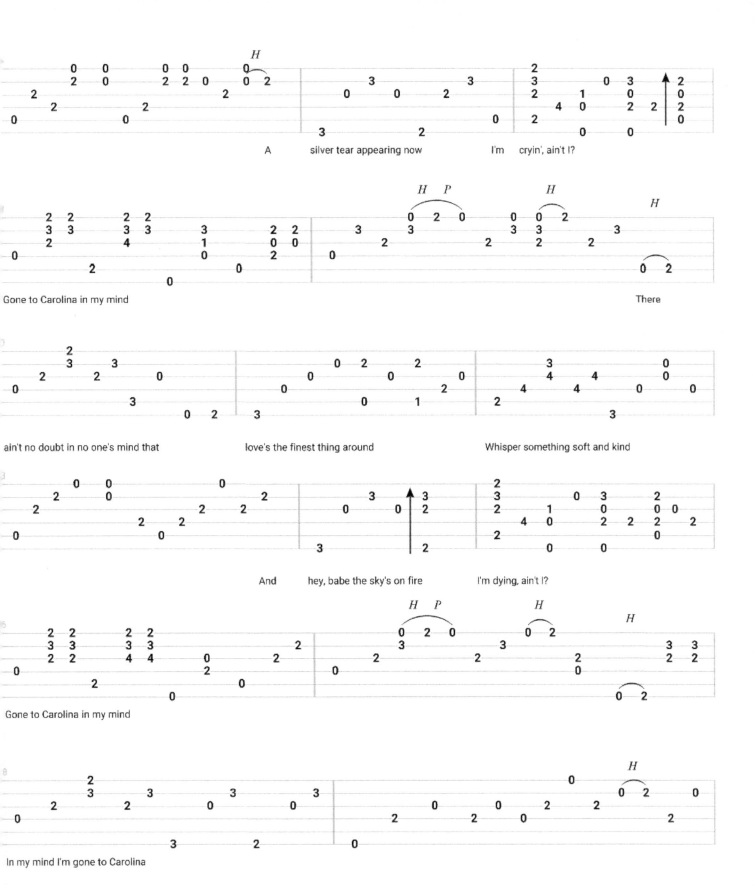

A   silver tear appearing now   I'm   cryin', ain't I?

Gone to Carolina in my mind   There

ain't no doubt in no one's mind that   love's the finest thing around   Whisper something soft and kind

And   hey, babe the sky's on fire   I'm dying, ain't I?

Gone to Carolina in my mind

In my mind I'm gone to Carolina

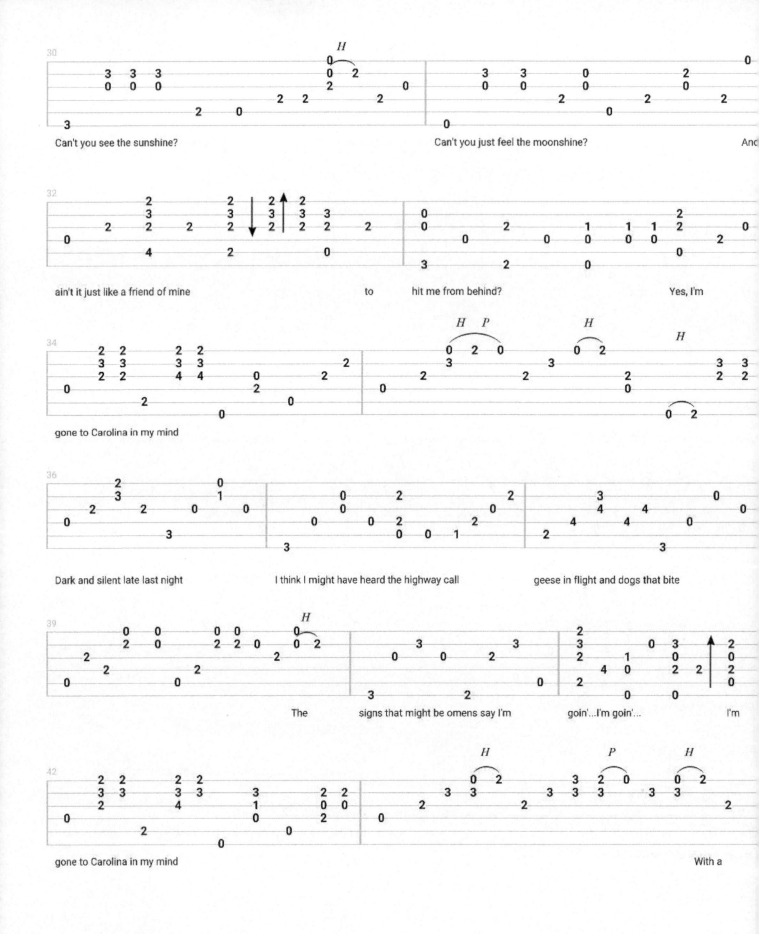

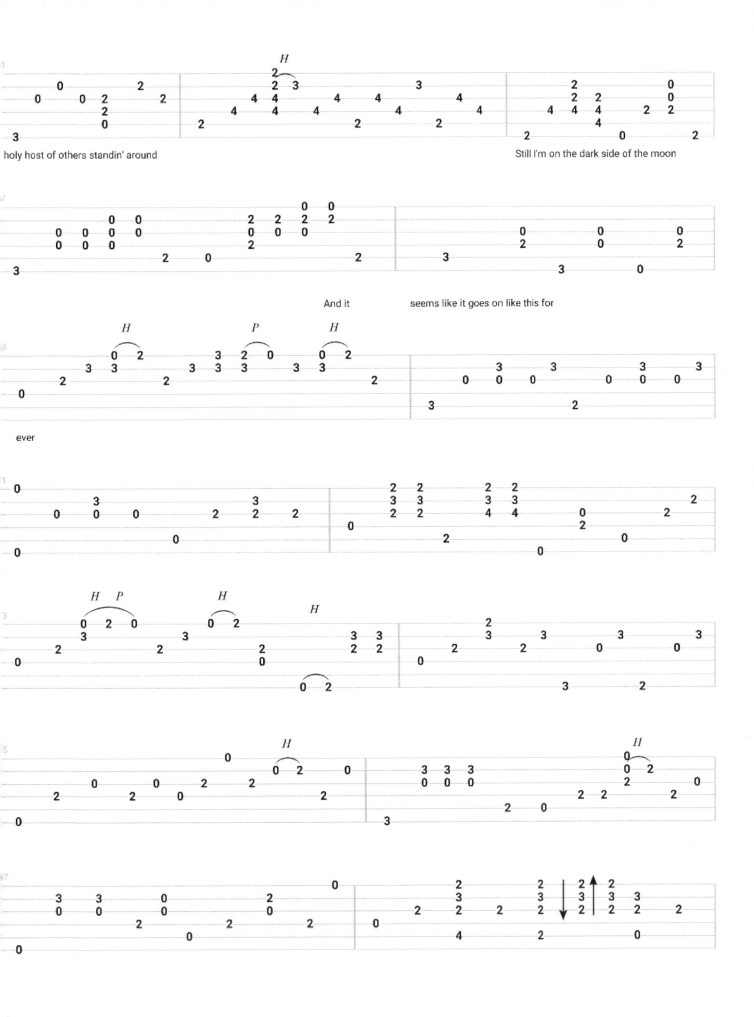

holy host of others standin' around

Still I'm on the dark side of the moon

And it   seems like it goes on like this for

ever

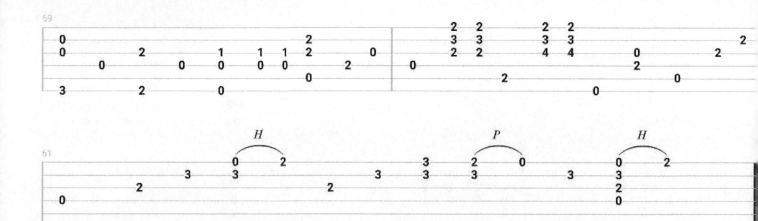

Caroline I See You
James Taylor

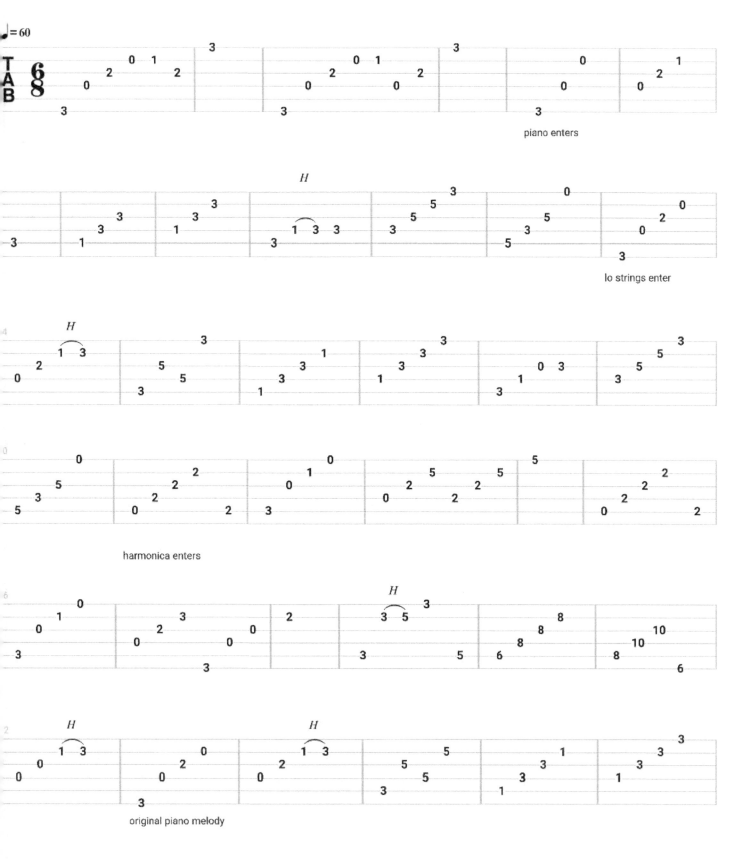

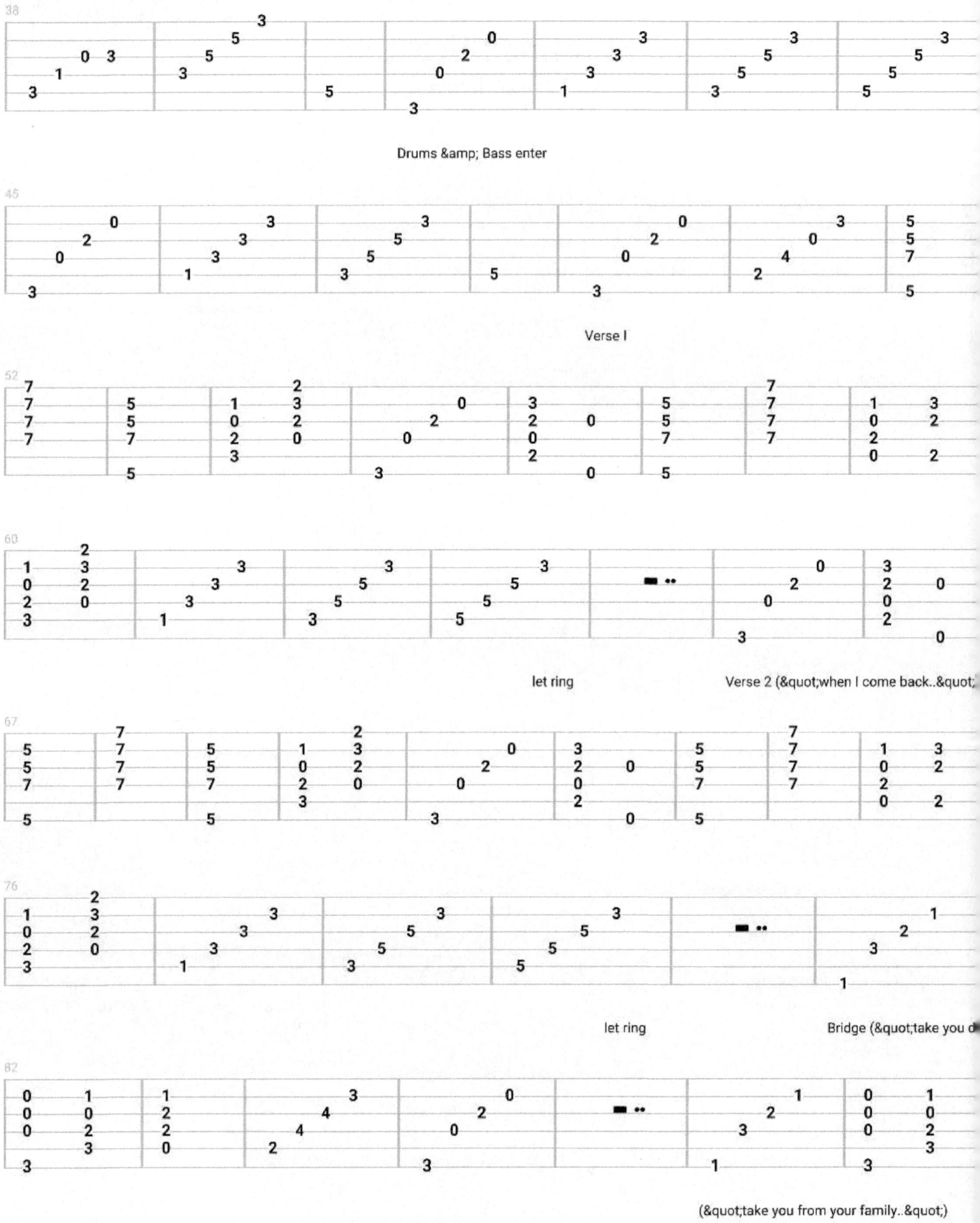

Drums & Bass enter

Verse I

let ring

Verse 2 ("when I come back..")

let ring

Bridge ("take you o

("take you from your family..")

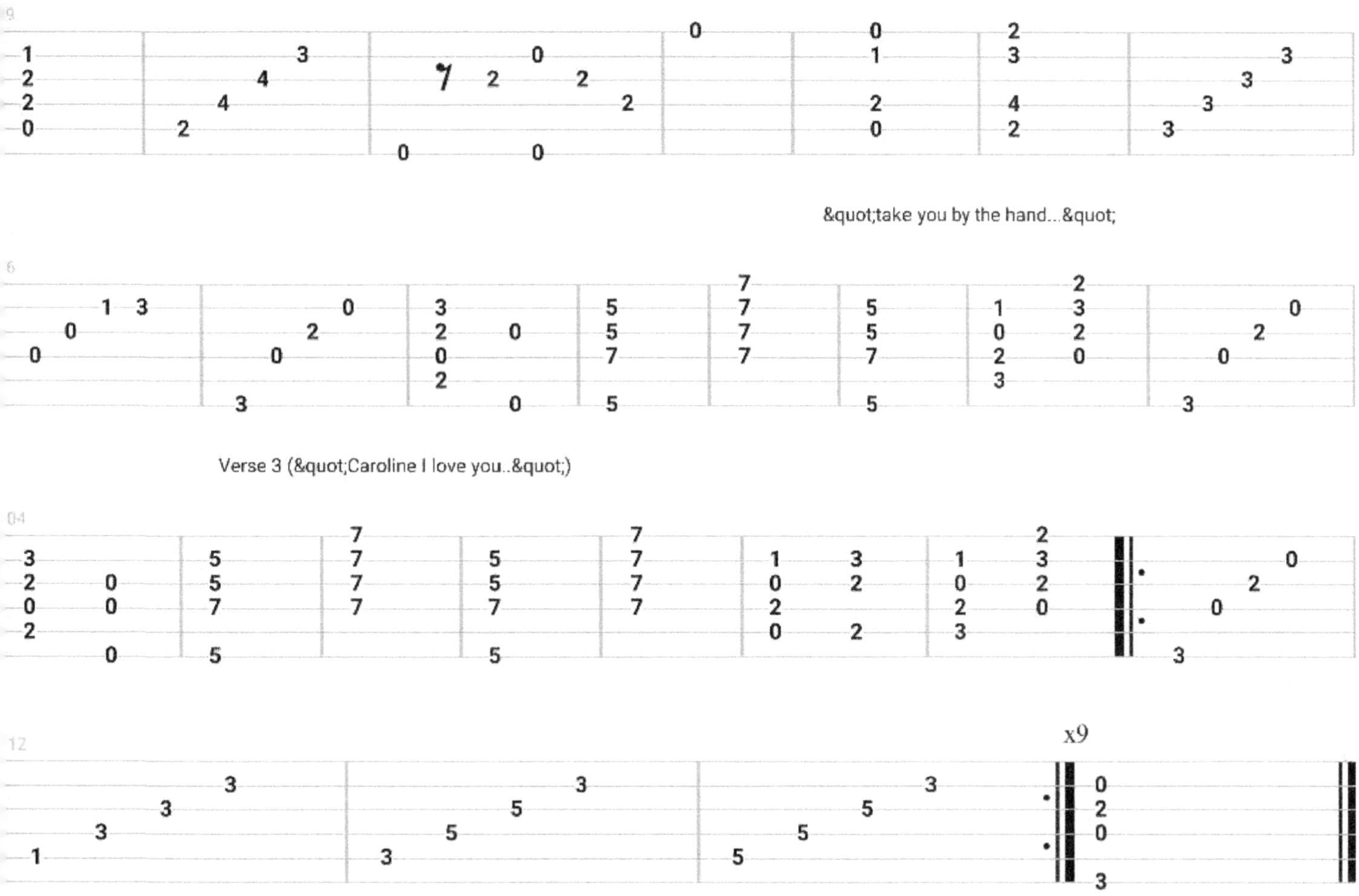

"take you by the hand..."

Verse 3 ("Caroline I love you..")

x9

Country Road

James Taylor

Tuning: D A D G B E

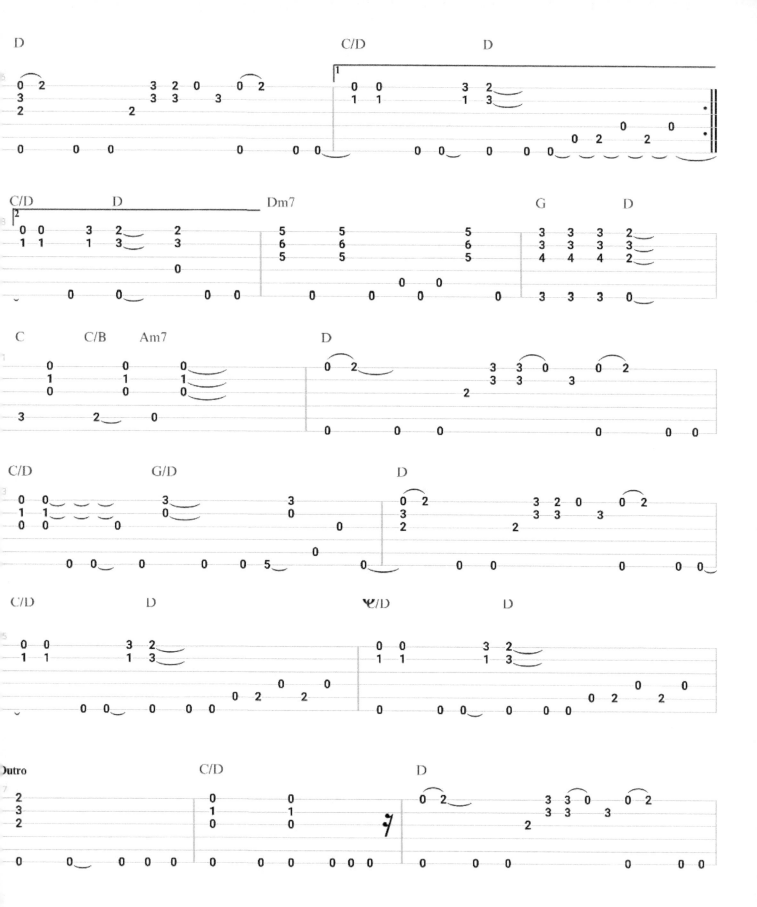

Dont Let Me Be Lonely Tonight

James Taylor

Tuning: E A D G B E

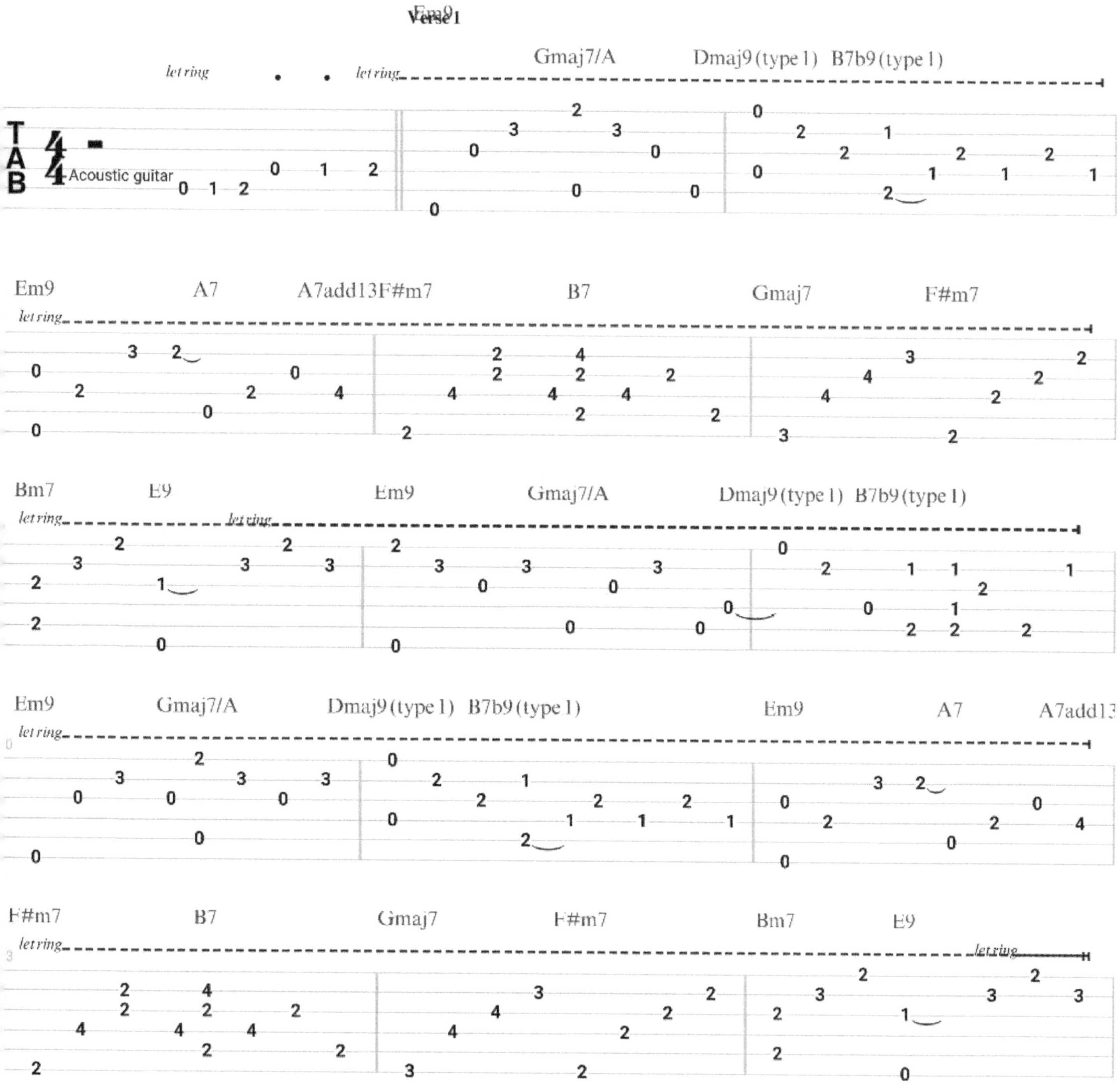

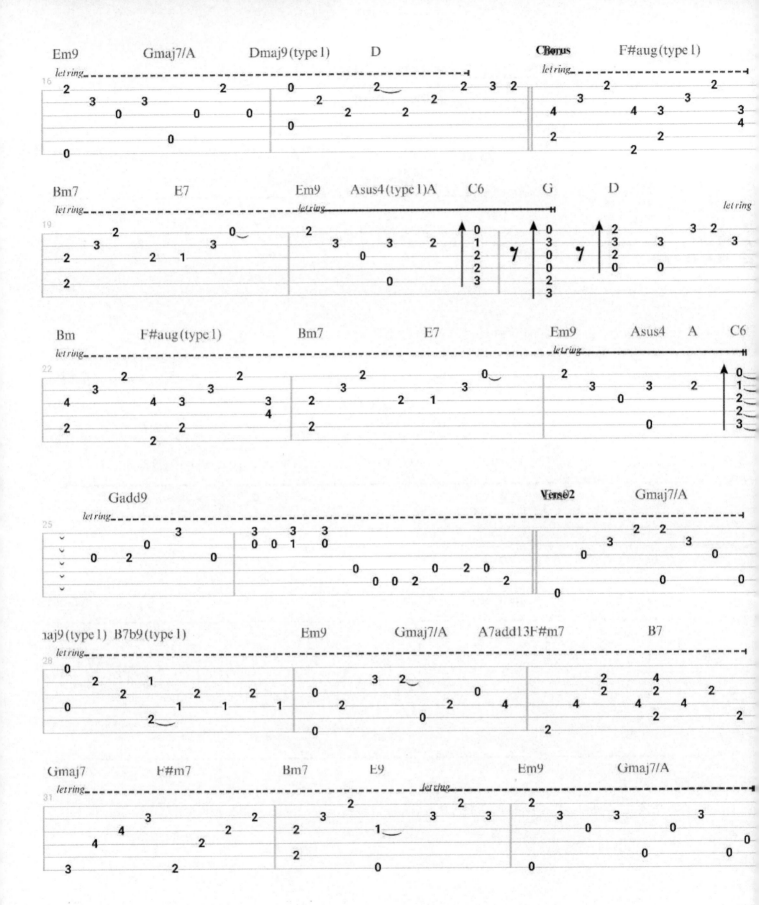

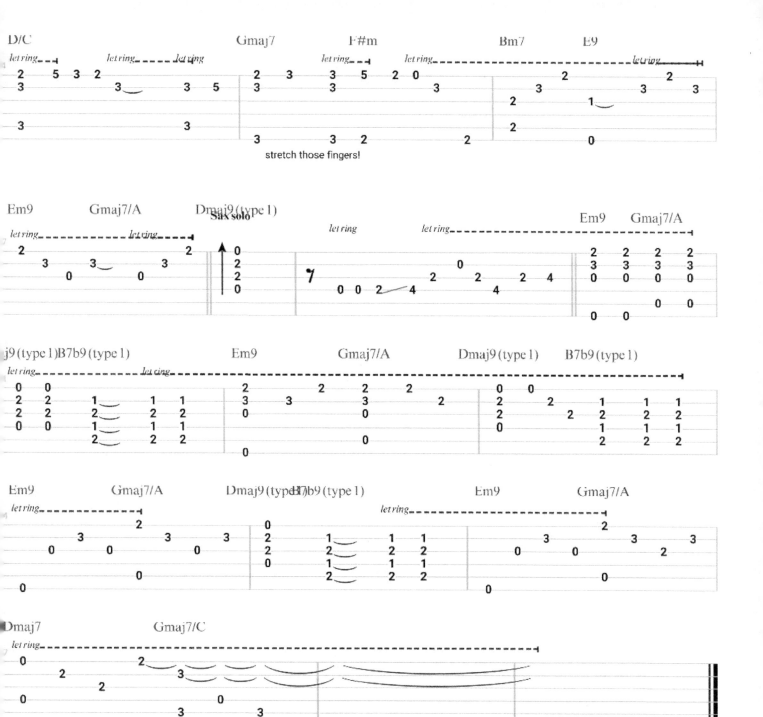

Fire And Rain

James Taylor

Tuning: E A D G B E

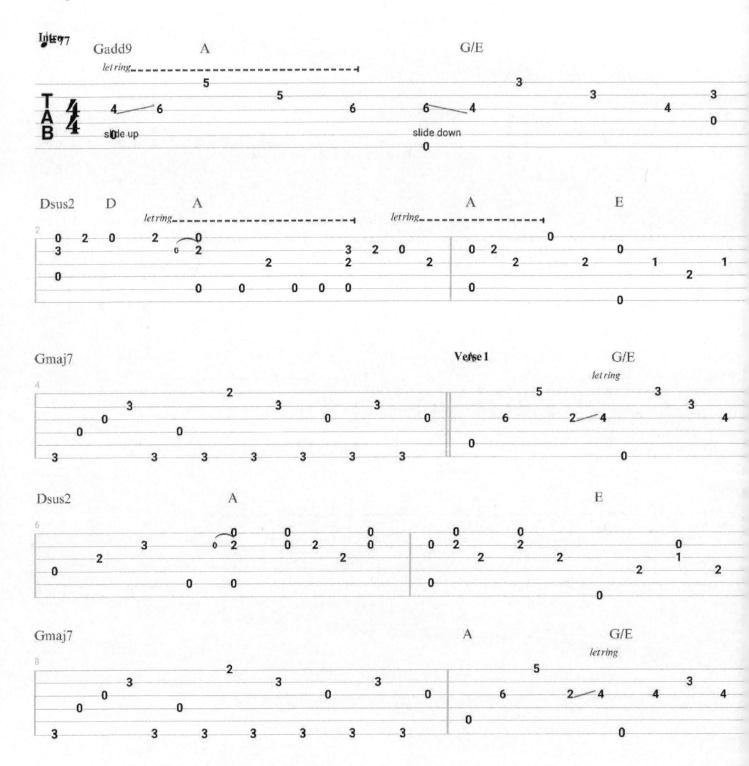

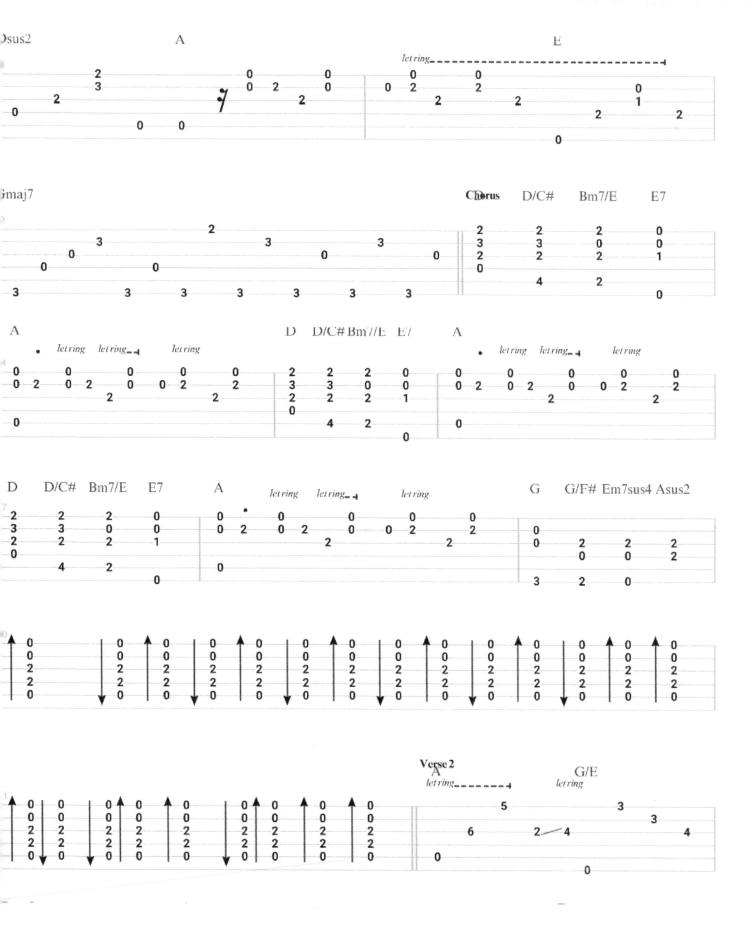

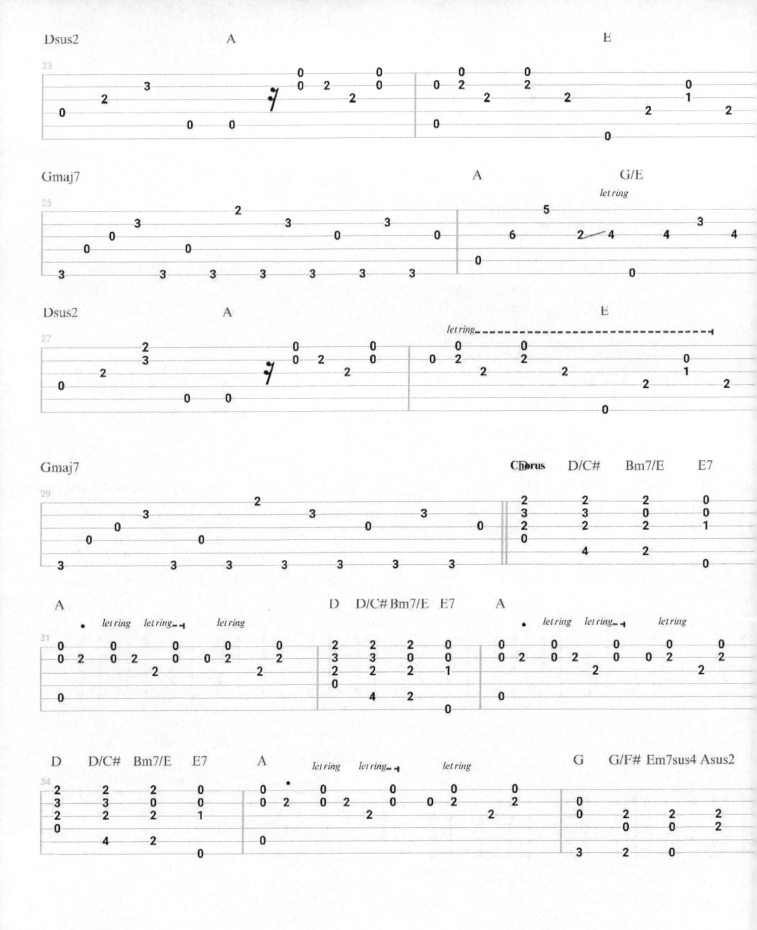

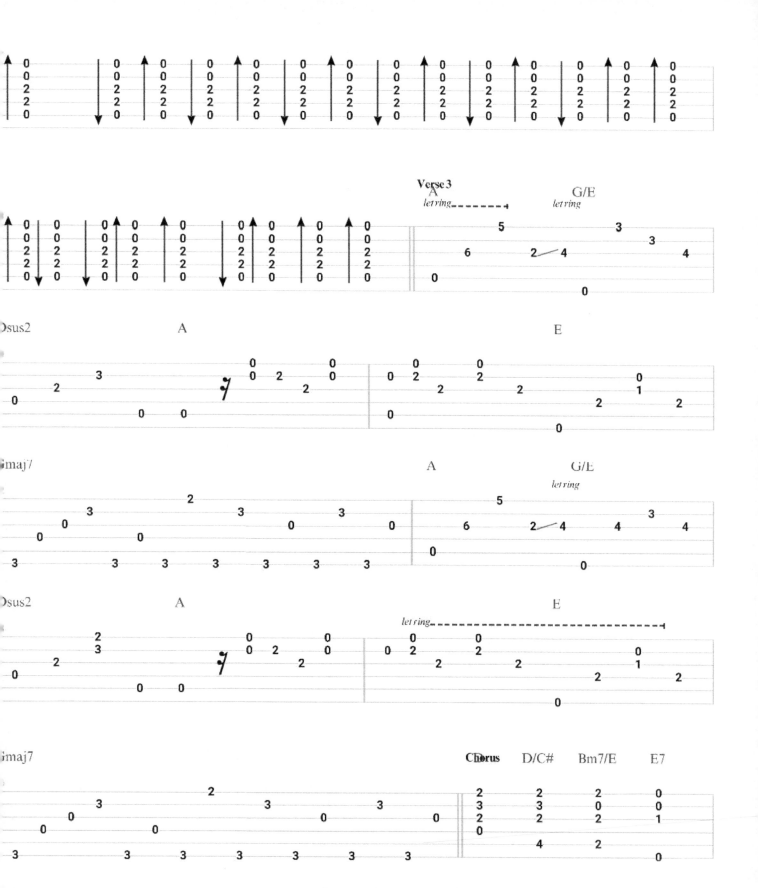

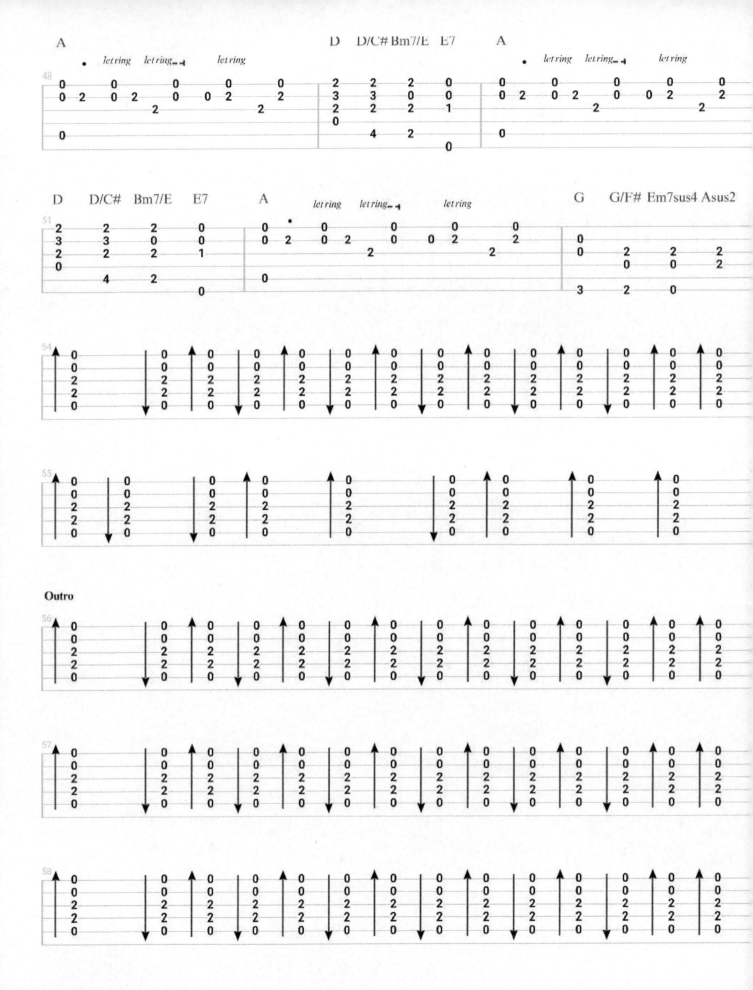

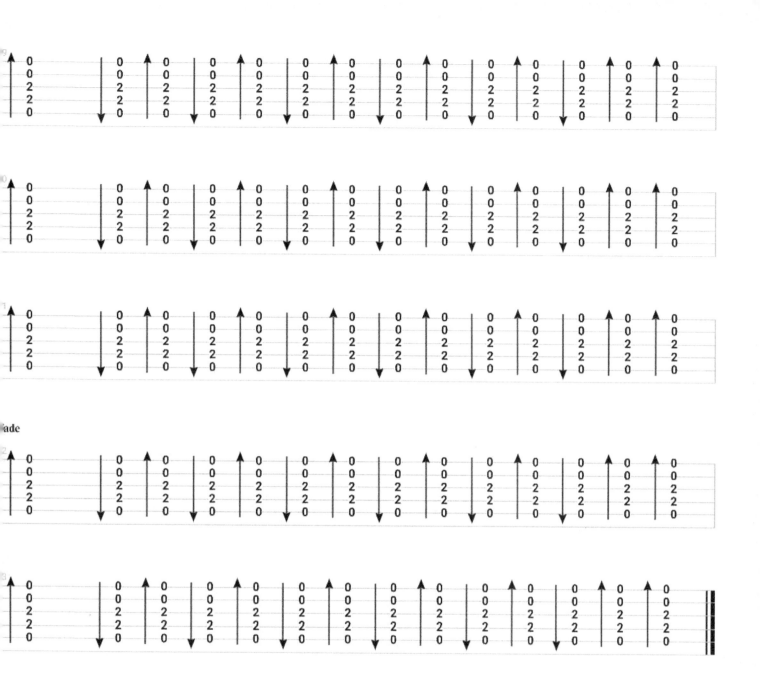

God Rest Ye Merry Gentlemen
James Taylor

Tuning: E A D G B E

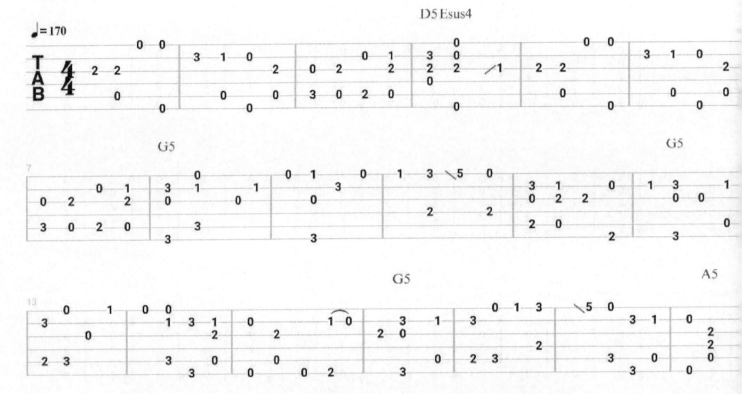

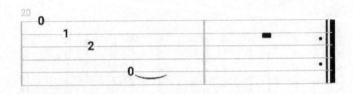

Handy Man
James Taylor

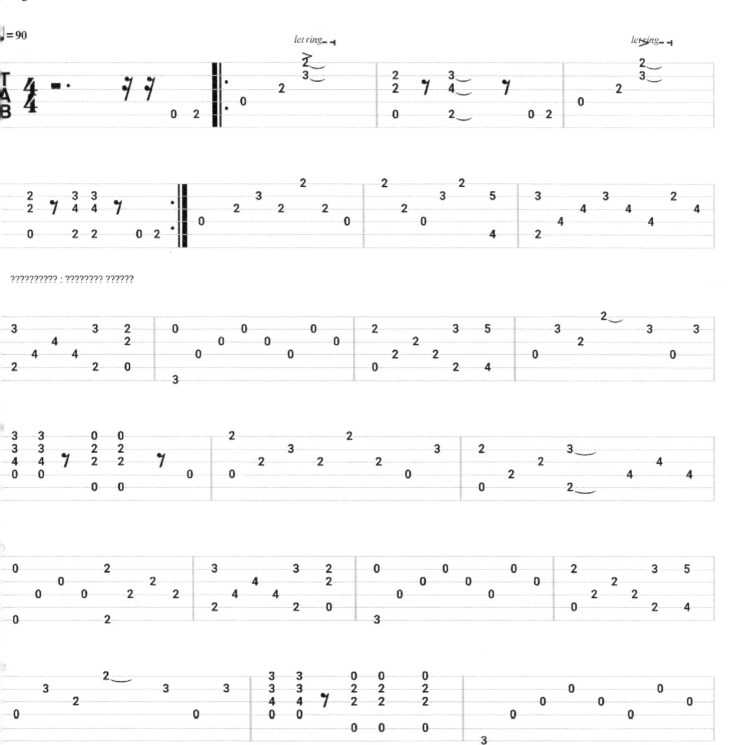

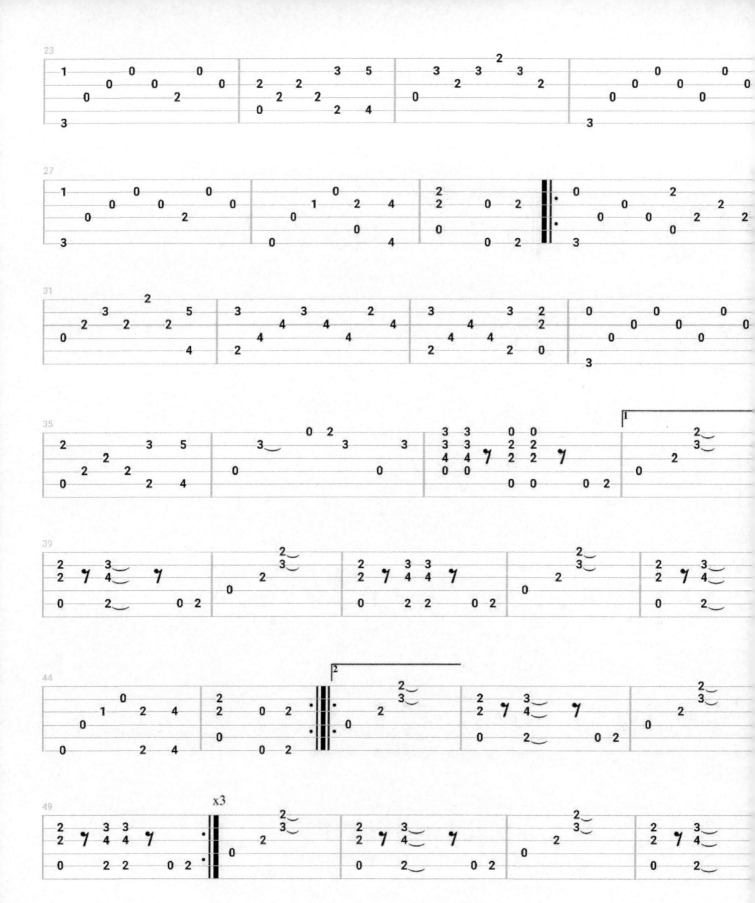

Like Everyone She Knows
James Taylor

Tuning: E A D G B E

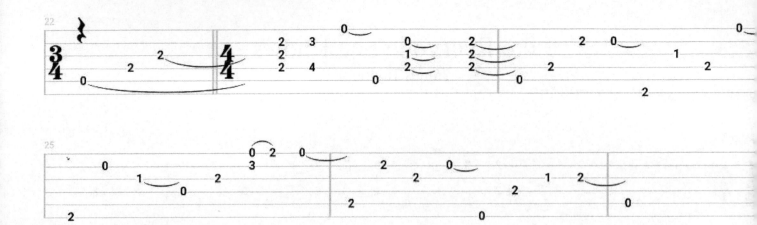

Long Ago And Far Away
James Taylor

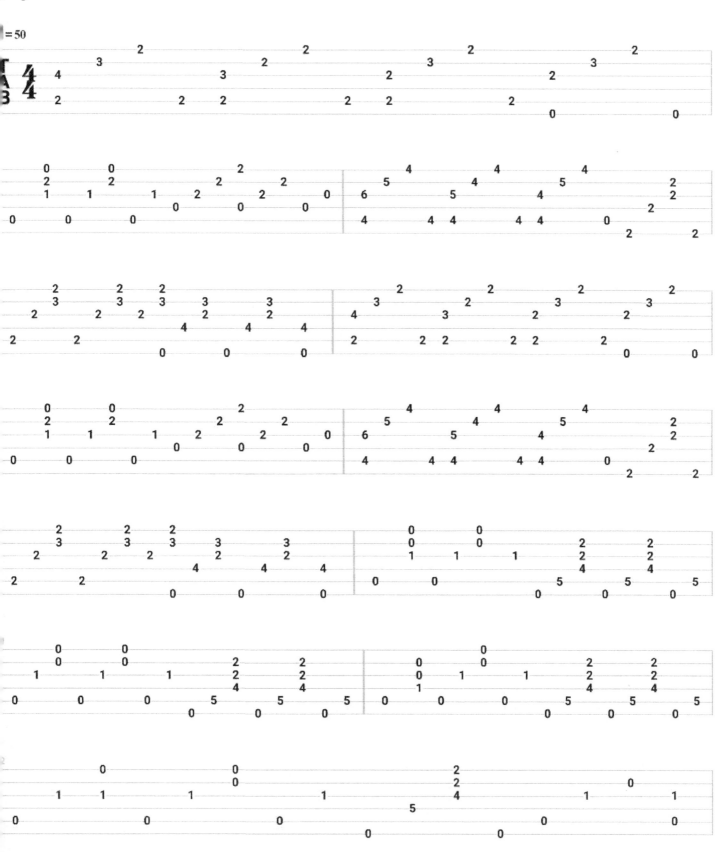

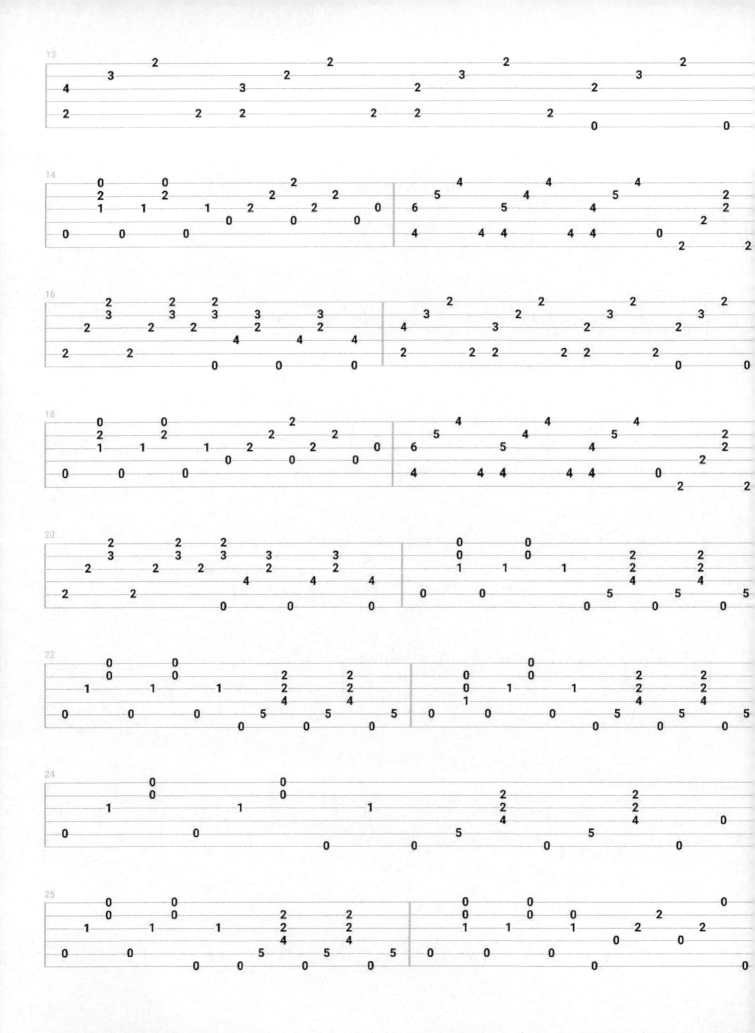

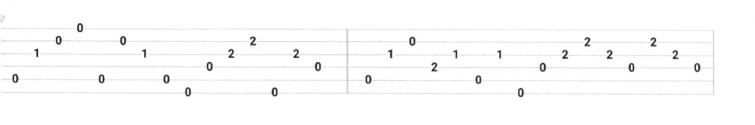

Mexico
James Taylor

Tuning: E A D G B E

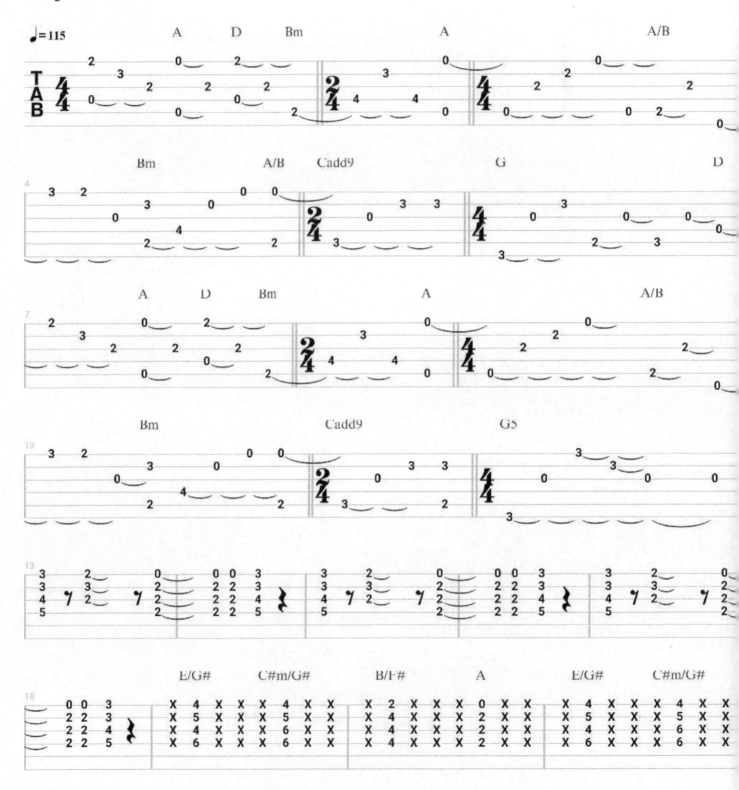

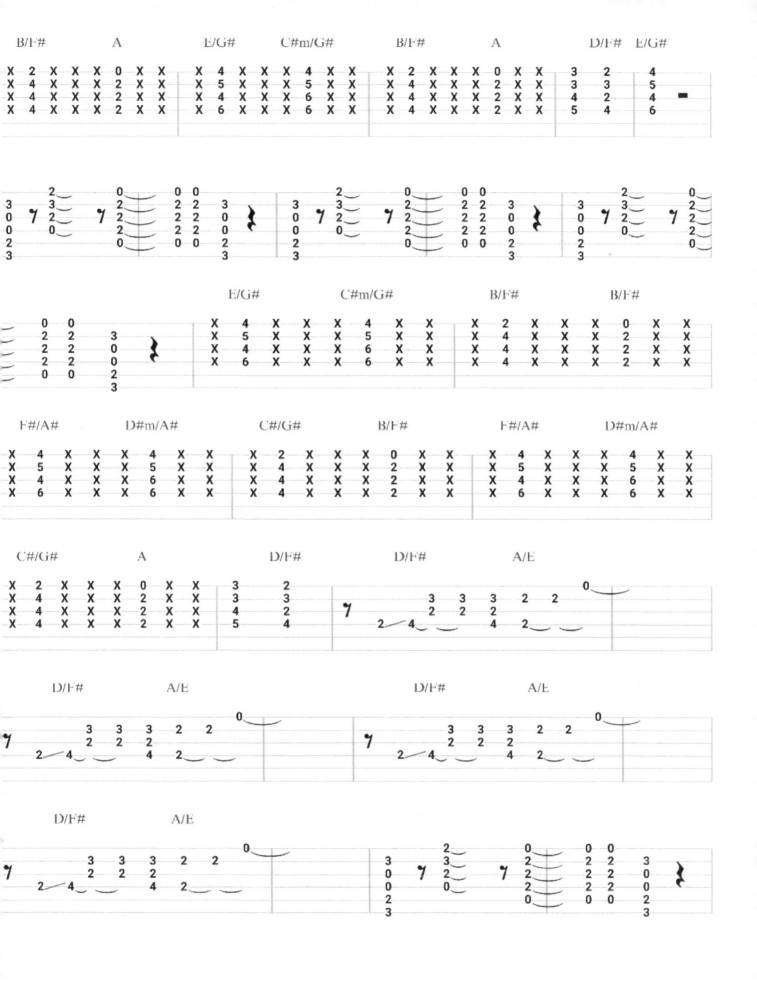

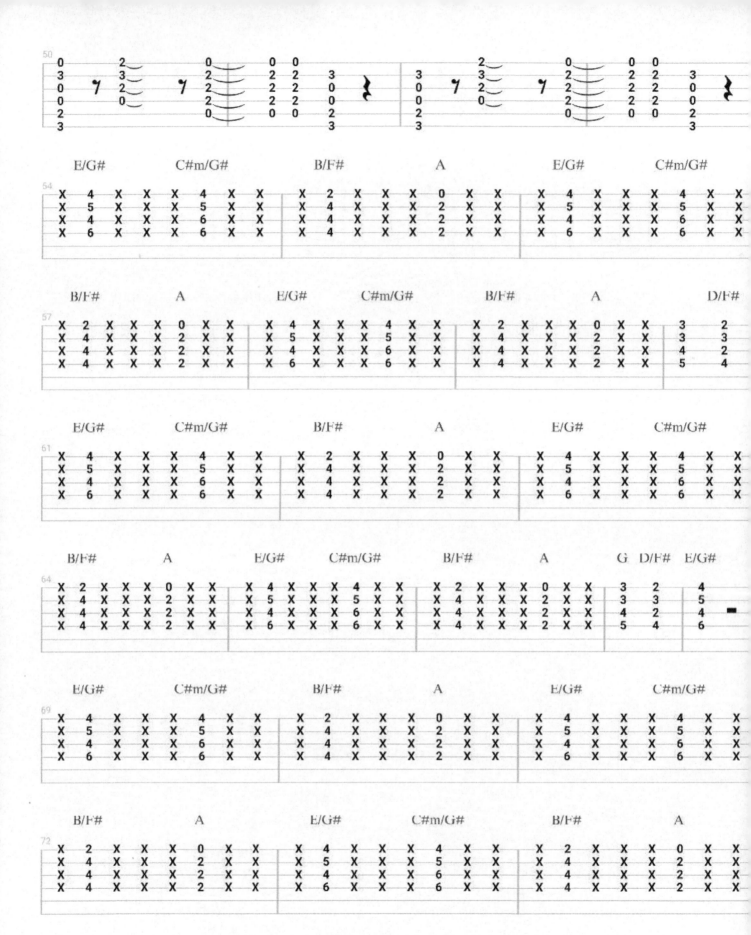

```
        E/G#              C#m/G#            |     B/F#              A
X---4---X---X---X---4---X---X---|---X---2---X---X---X---0---X---X---||
X---5---X---X---X---5---X---X---|---X---4---X---X---X---2---X---X---||
X---4---X---X---X---6---X---X---|---X---4---X---X---X---2---X---X---||
X---6---X---X---X---6---X---X---|---X---4---X---X---X---2---X---X---||
```

On The Fourth Of July

James Taylor

Tuning: E A D G B E

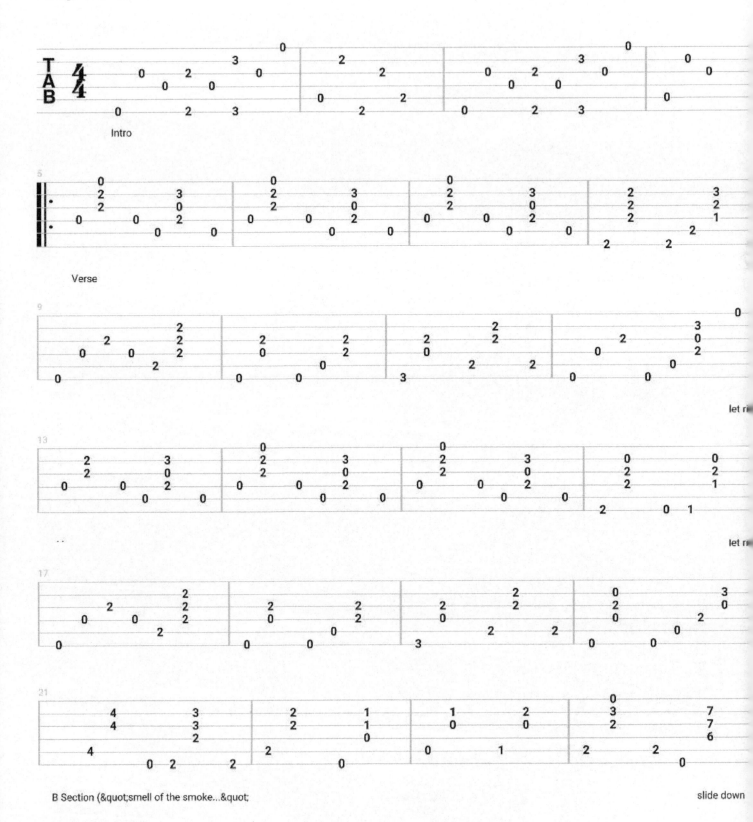

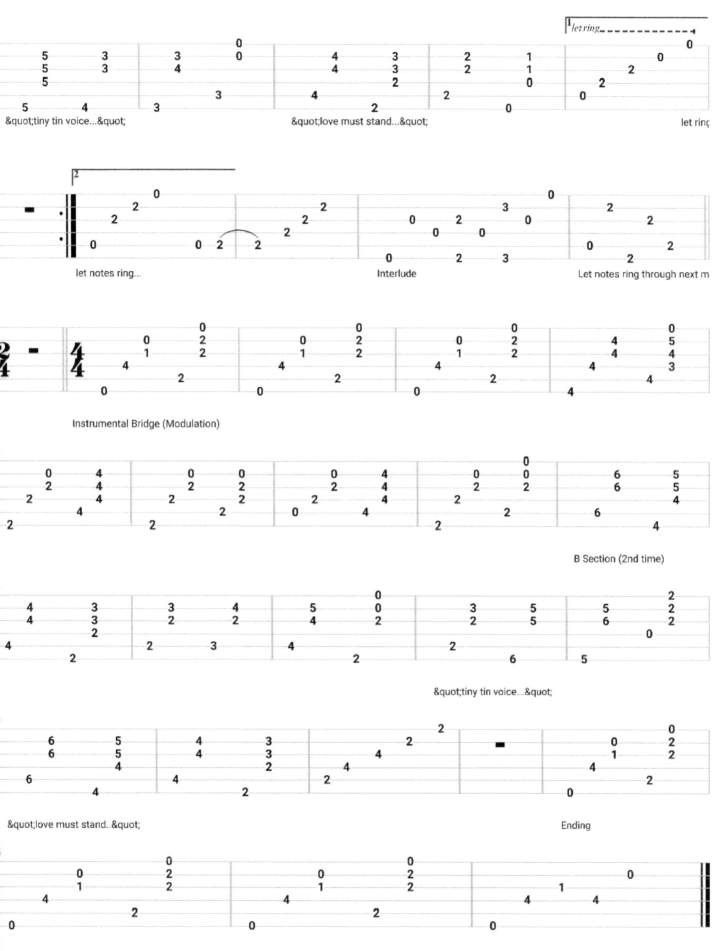

Sailing To Philadelphia
Mark Knopfler

Tuning: E A D G B E

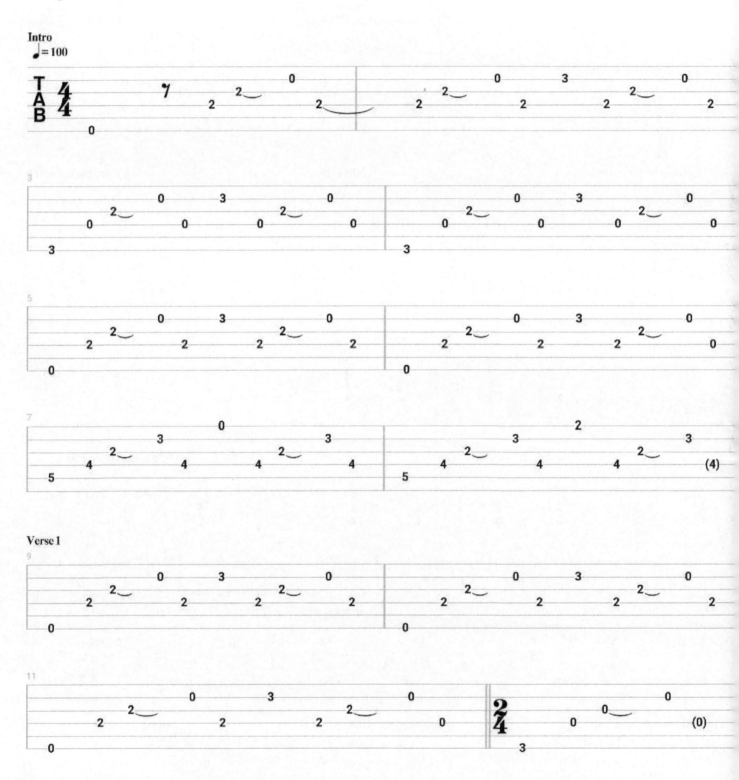

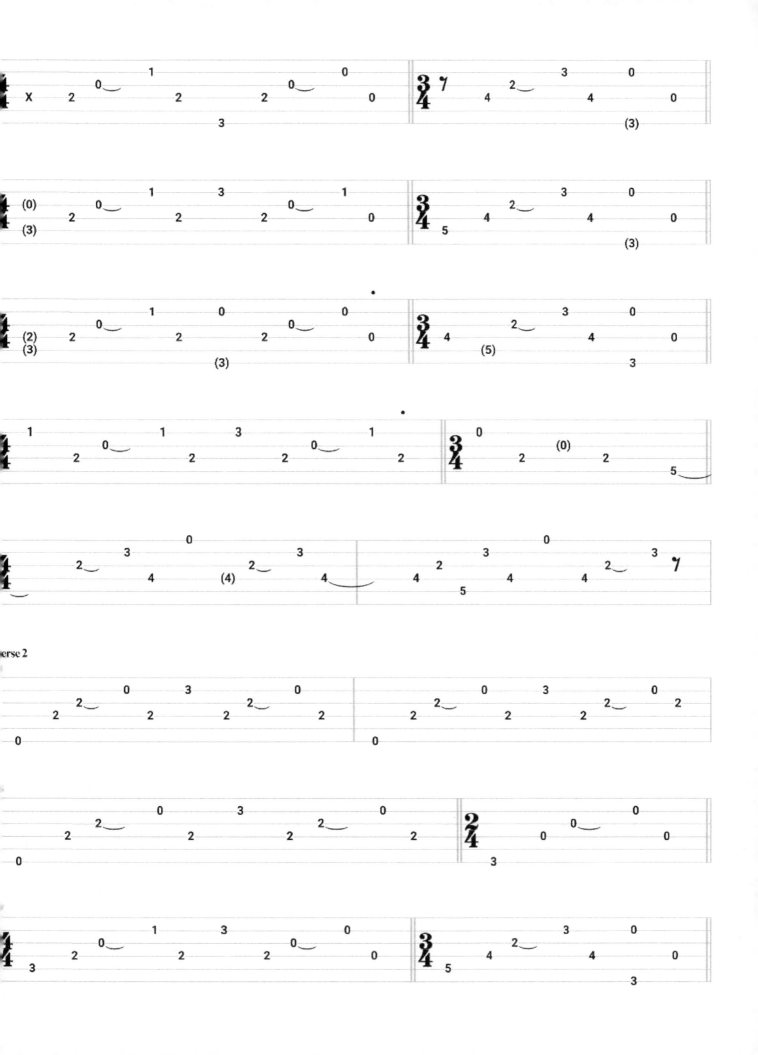

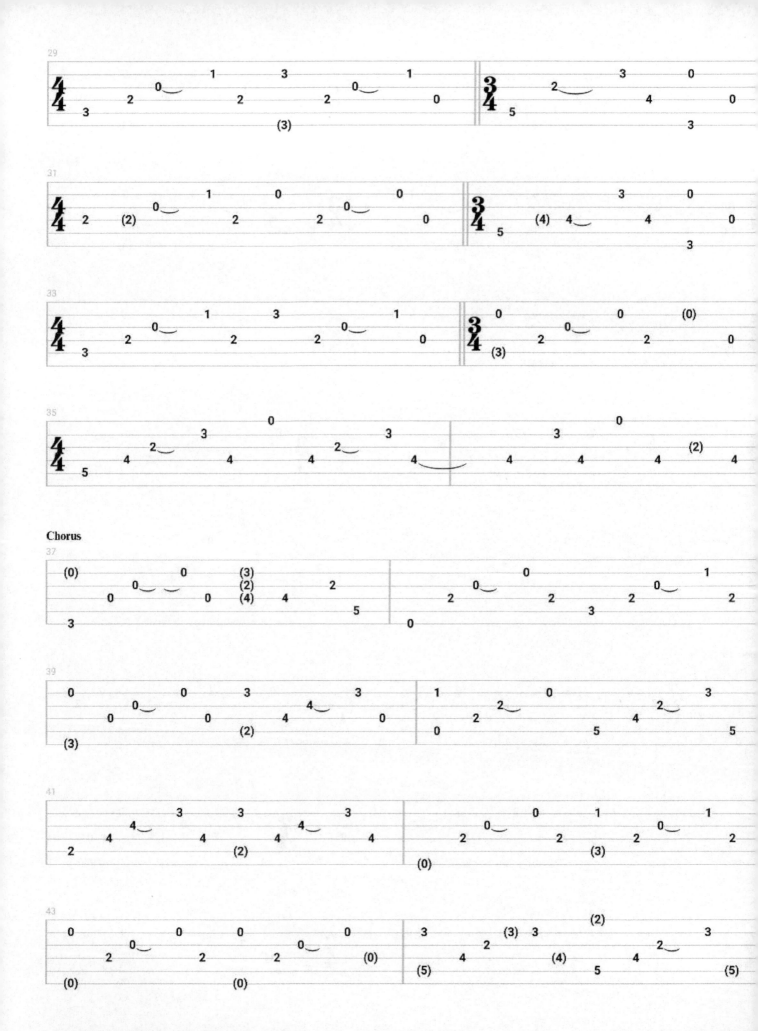

Chorus

Post-Chorus

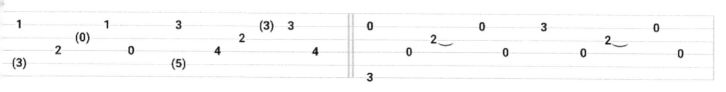

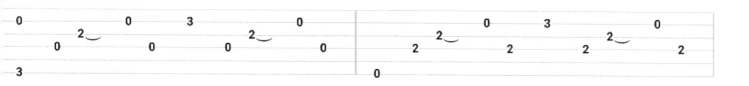

Verse 3

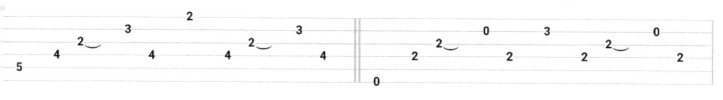

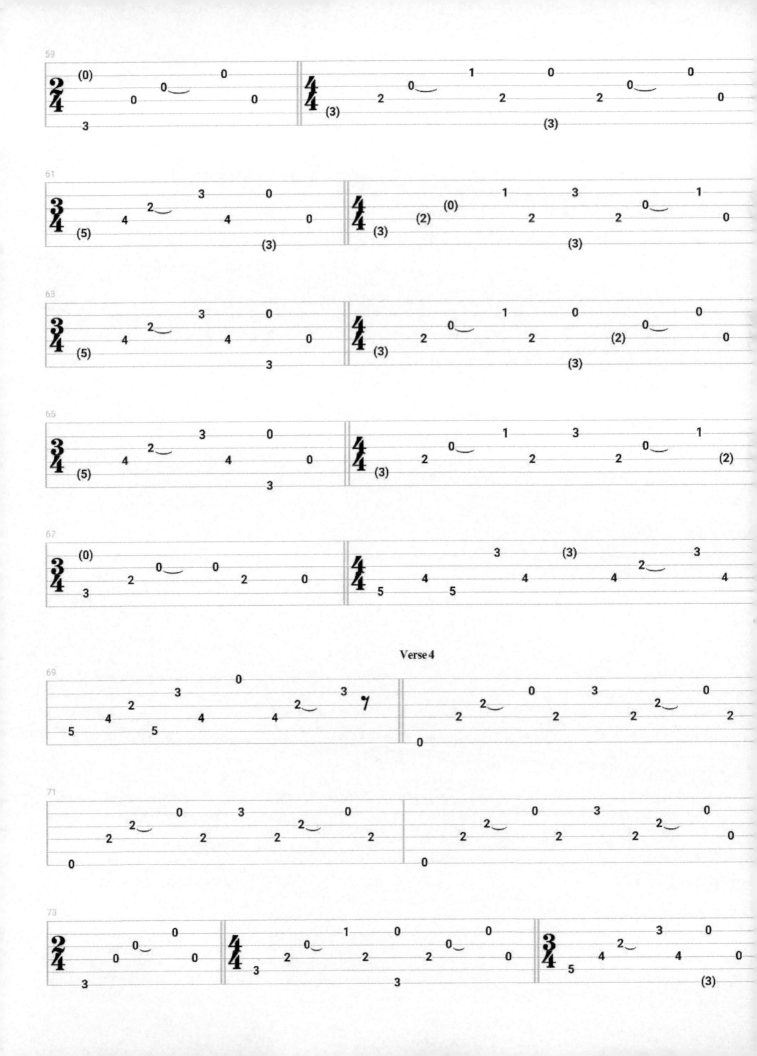

Verse 4

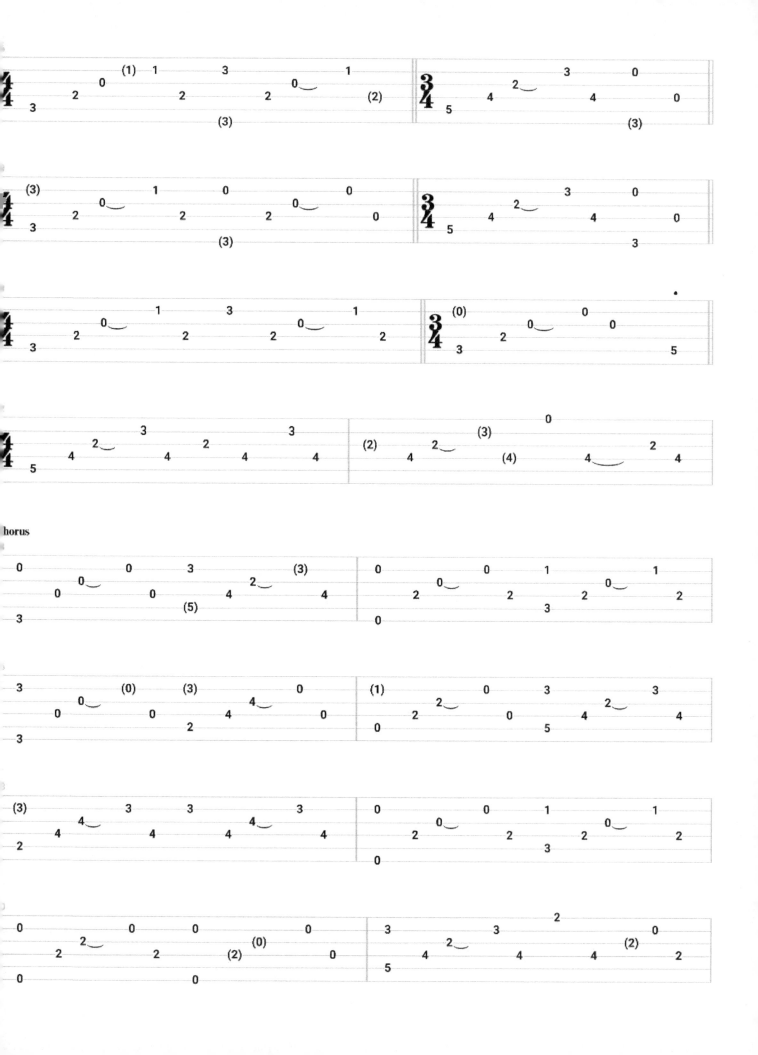

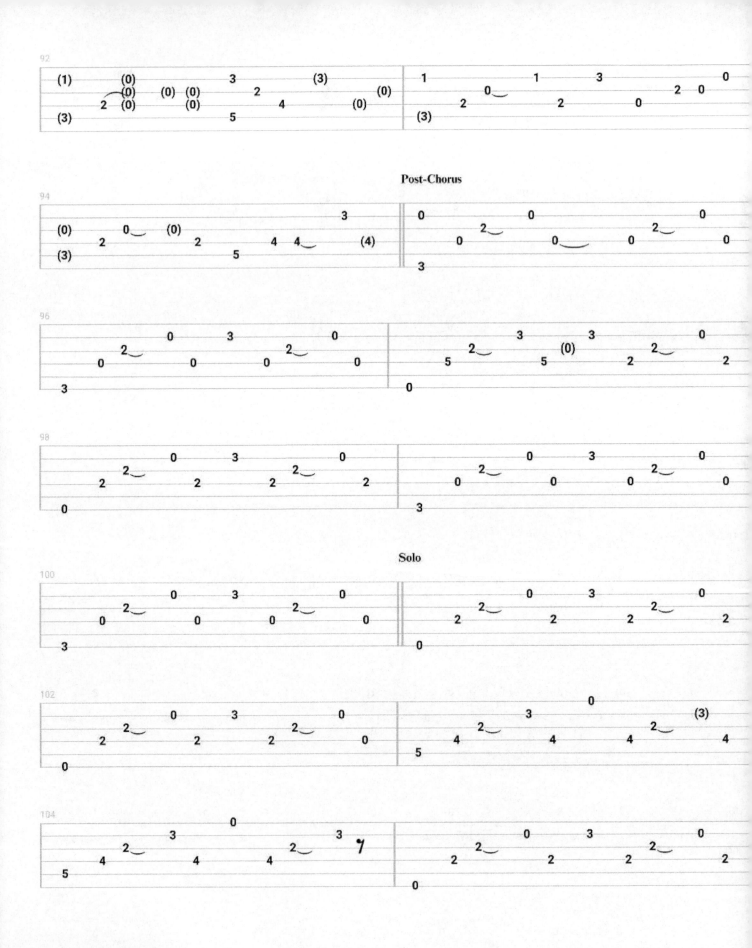

Post-Chorus

Solo

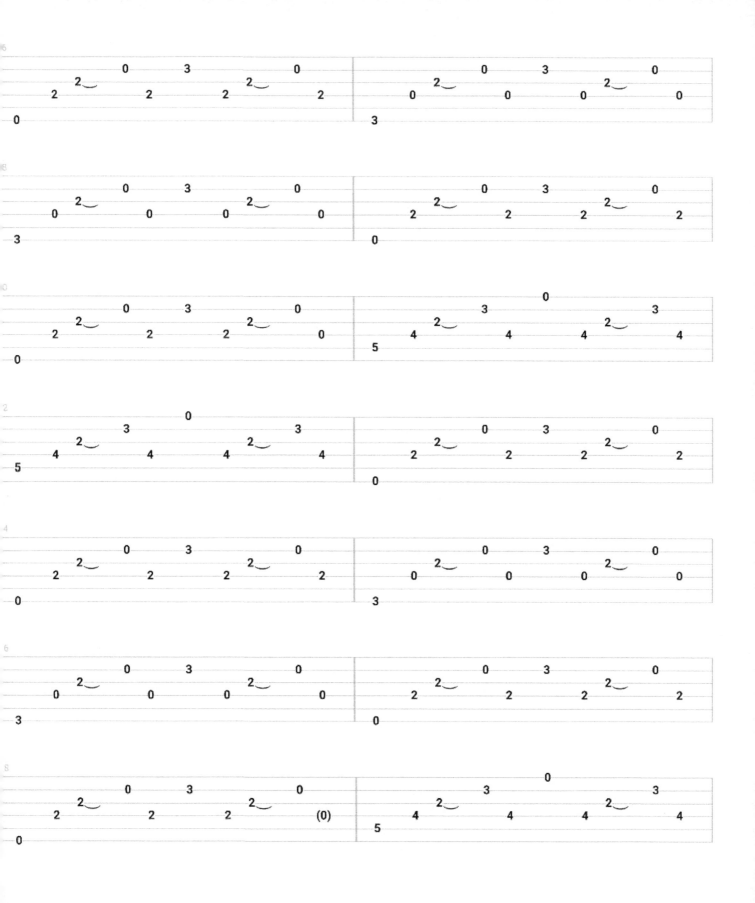

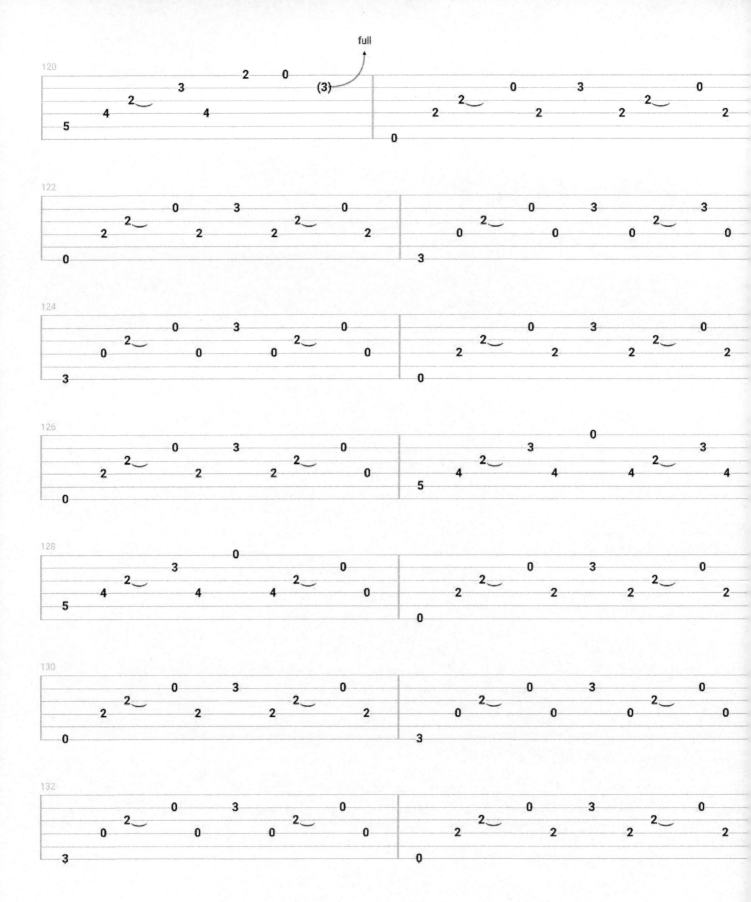

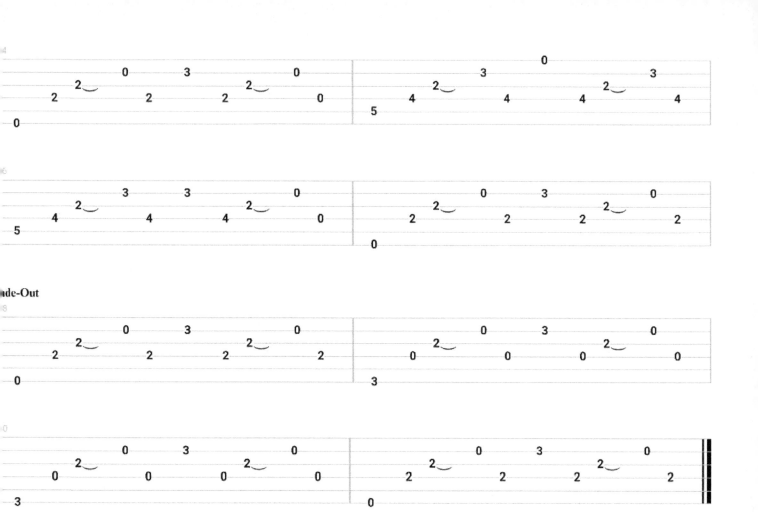

Secret Of Life

James Taylor

Tuning: E A D G B E

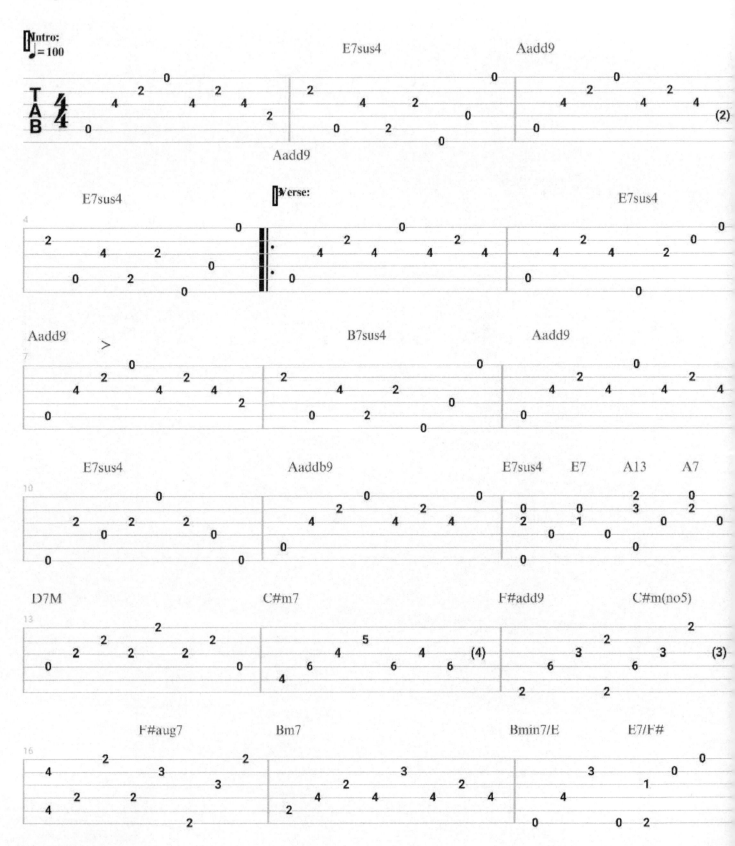

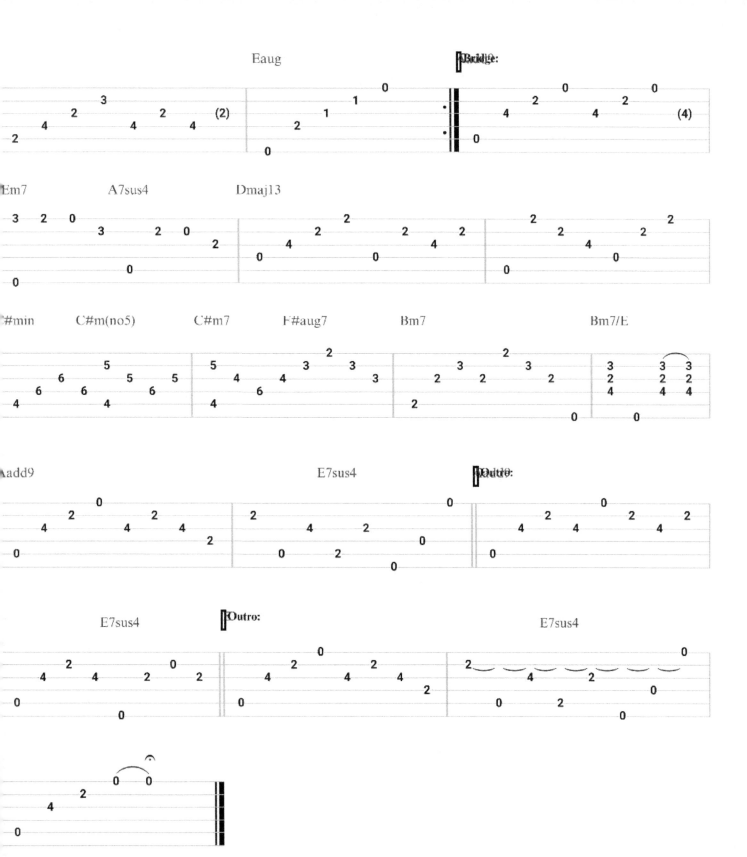

September Grass

James Taylor

Tuning: E A D G B E

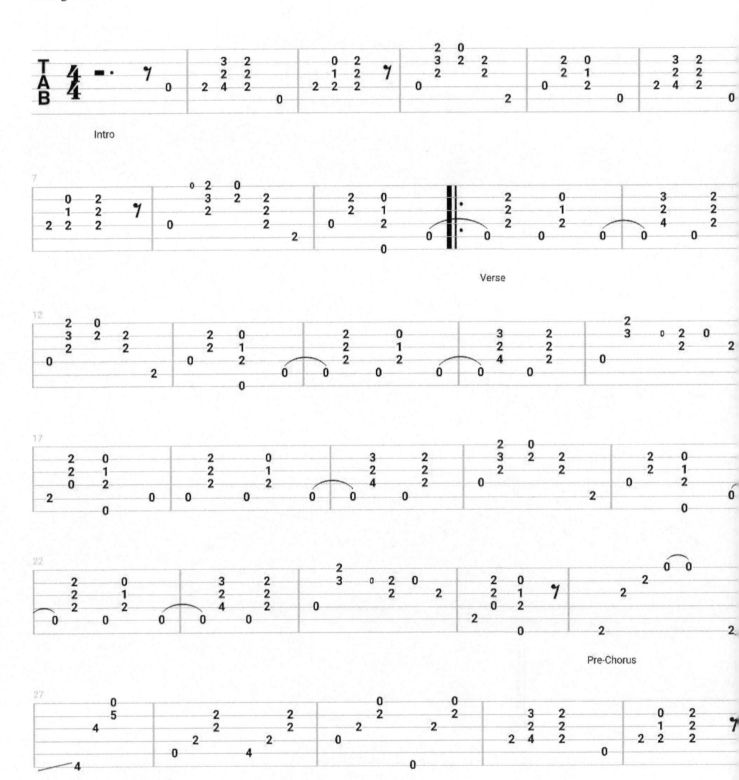

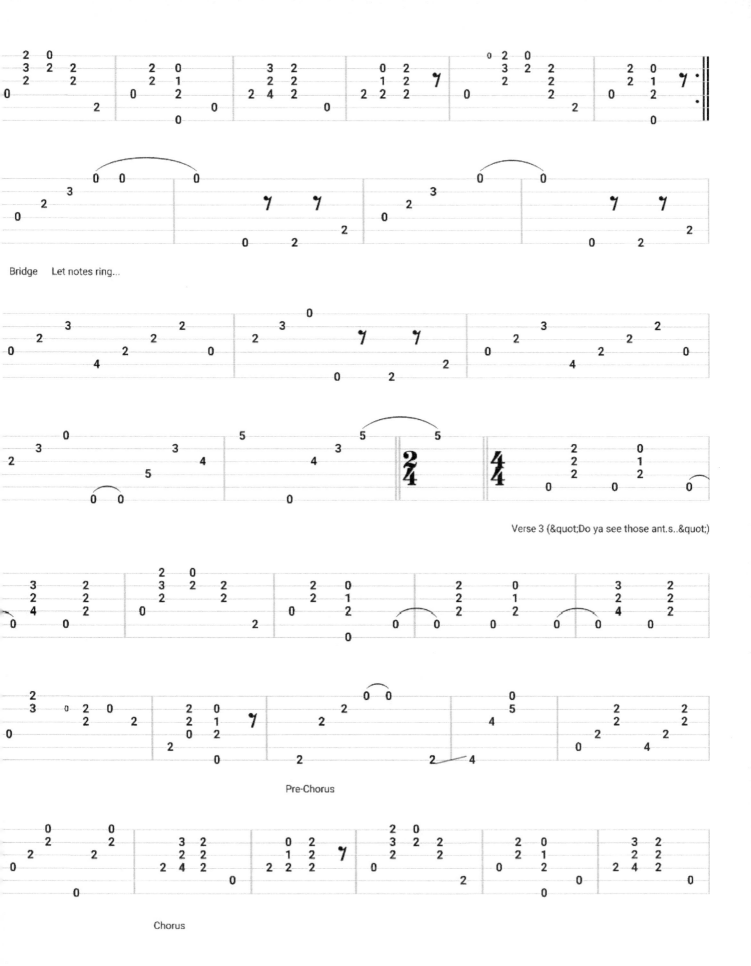

Bridge   Let notes ring...

Verse 3 ("Do ya see those ant.s..")

Pre-Chorus

Chorus

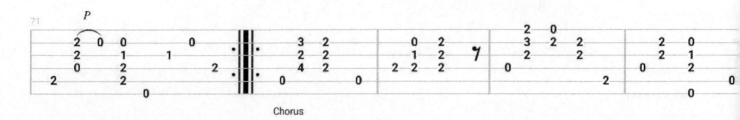

Interlude ("Lie Down...:")

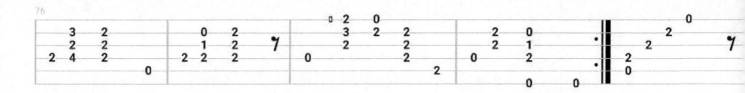

Chorus

Shower The People
James Taylor

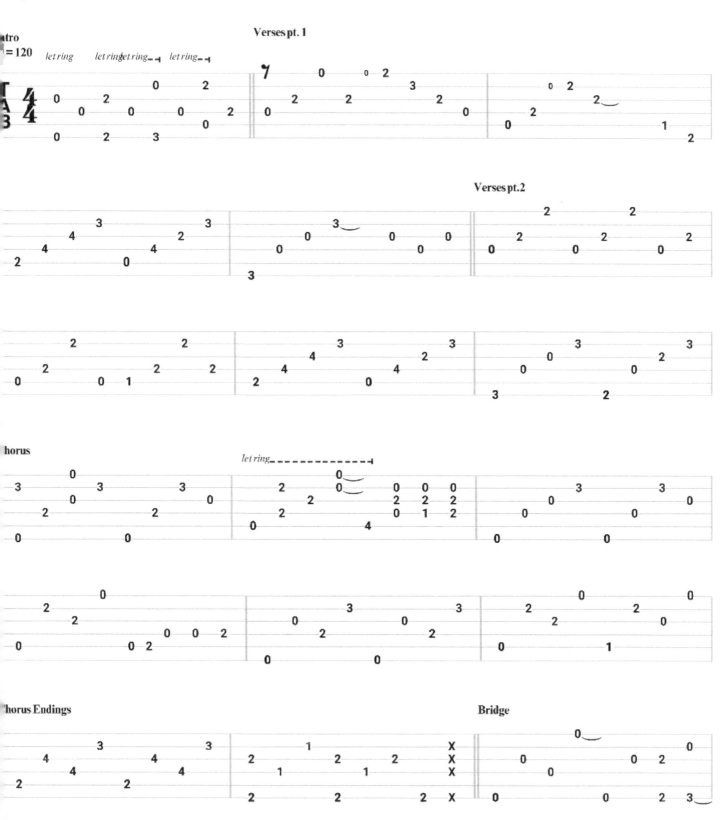

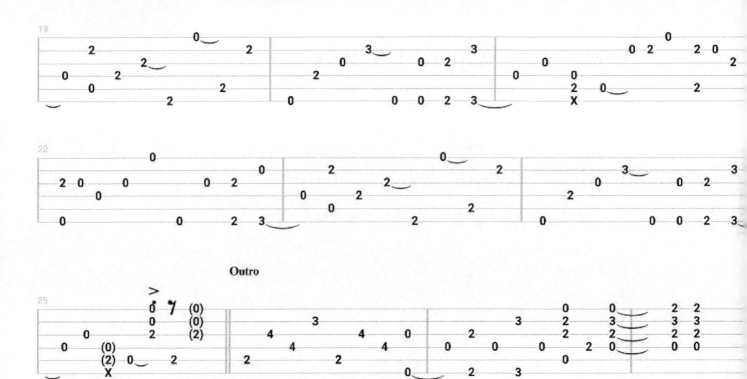

Outro

Something In The Way She Moves

James Taylor

Tuning: E A D G B E

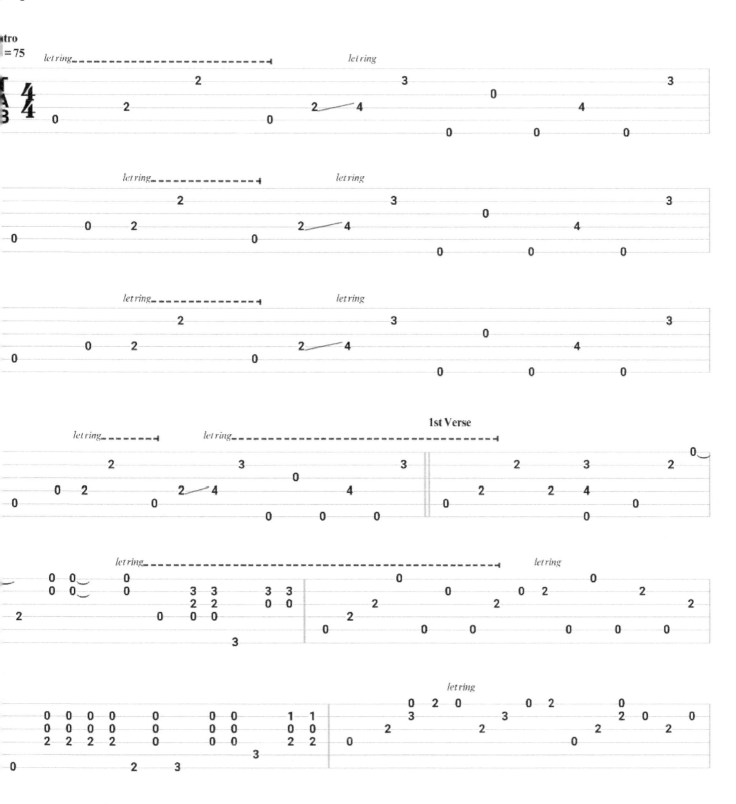

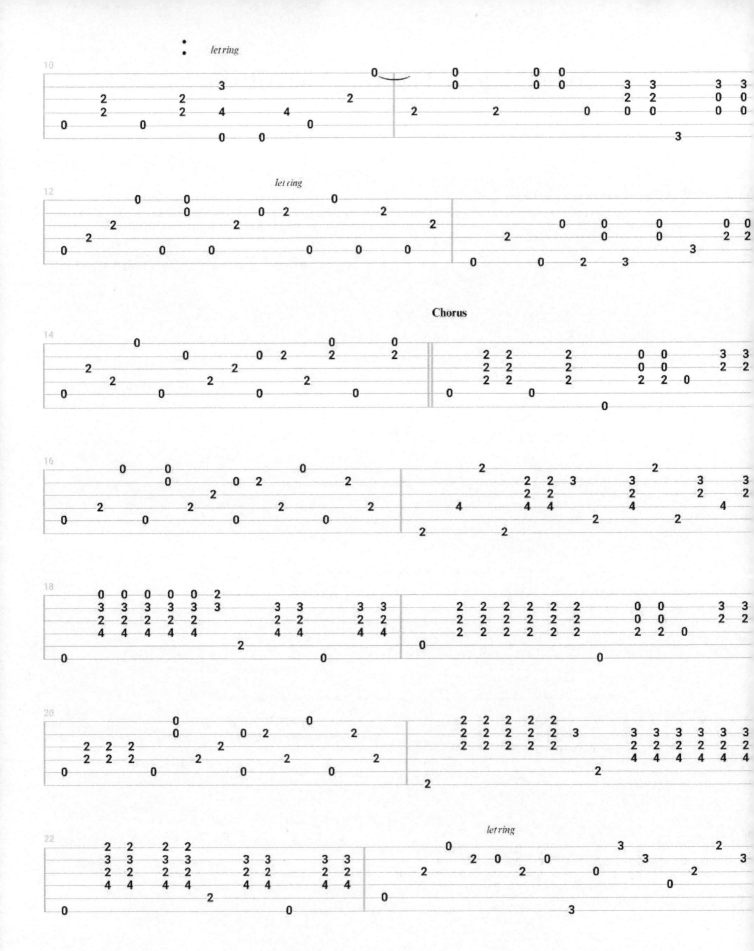

Interlude

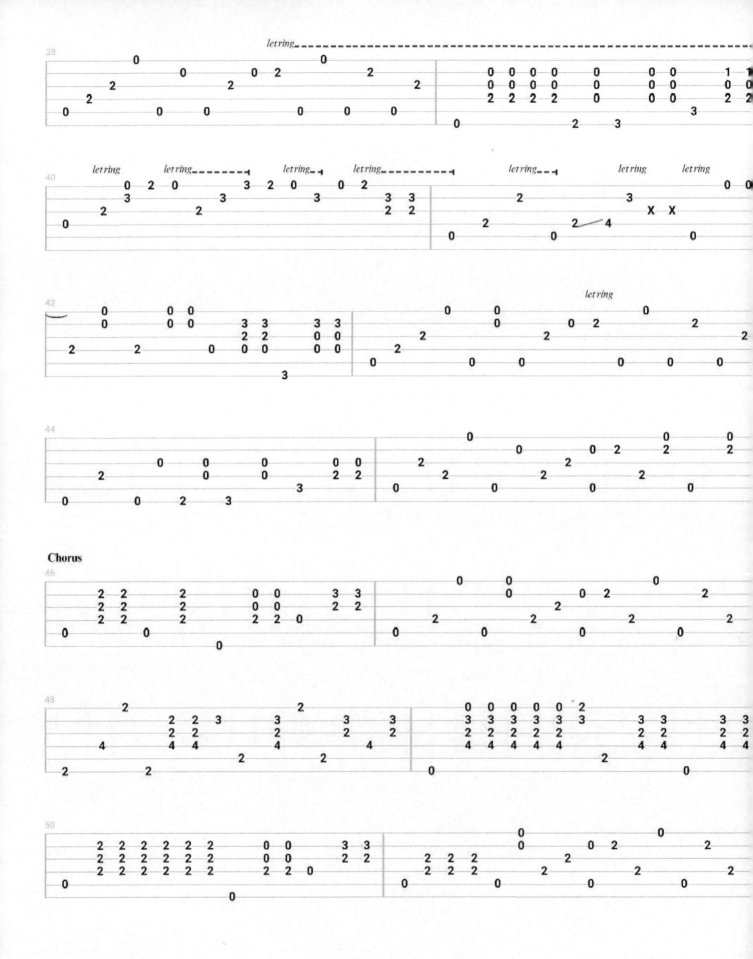

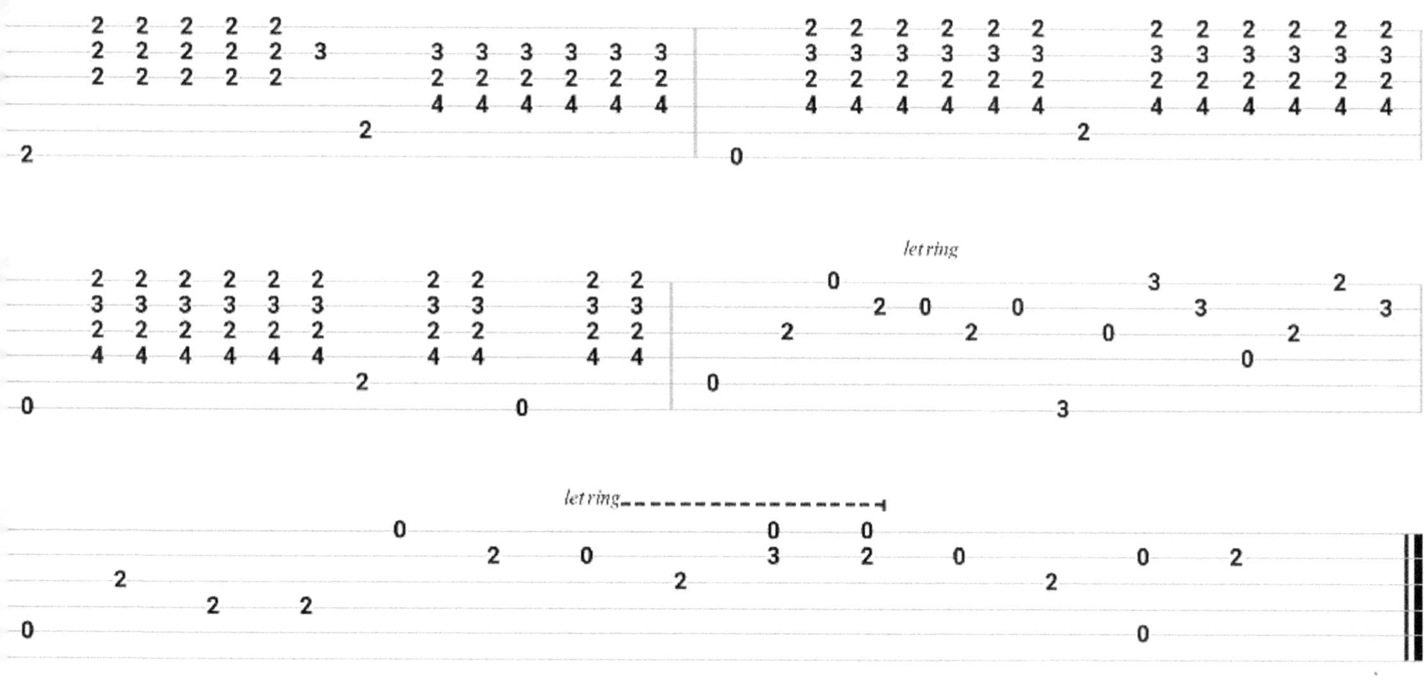
let ring
let ring

Steamroller
James Taylor

Tuning: E A D G B E

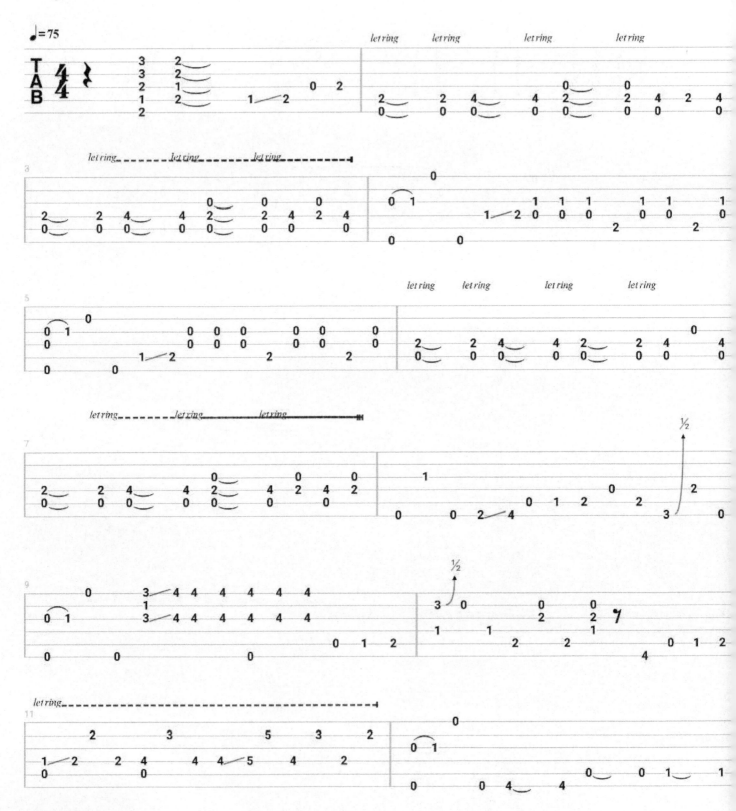

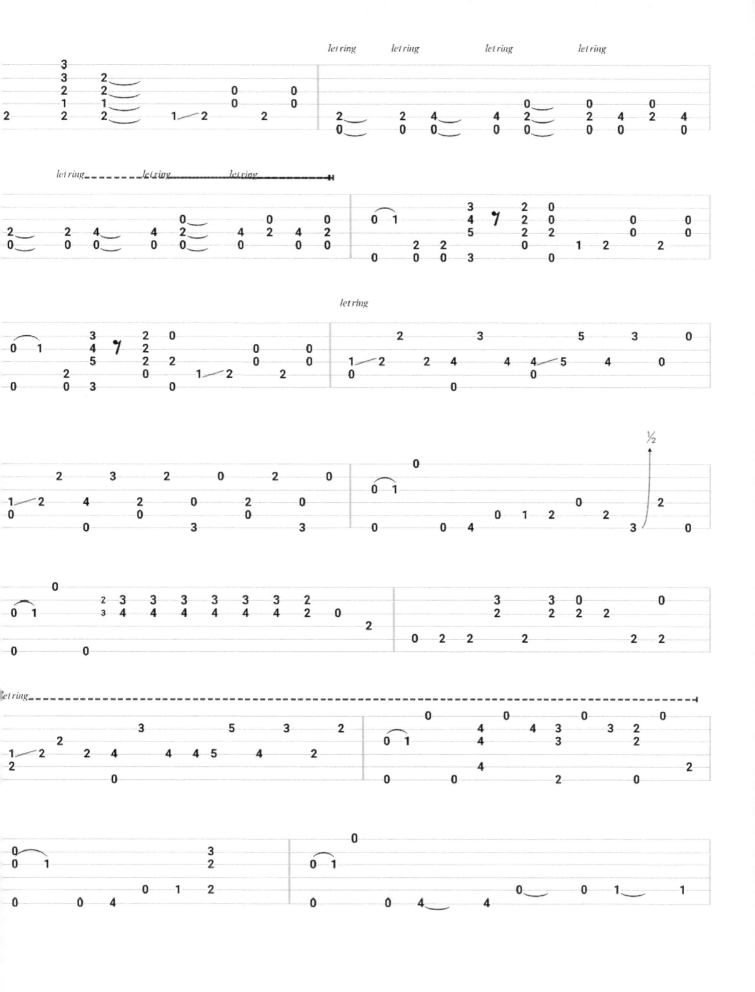

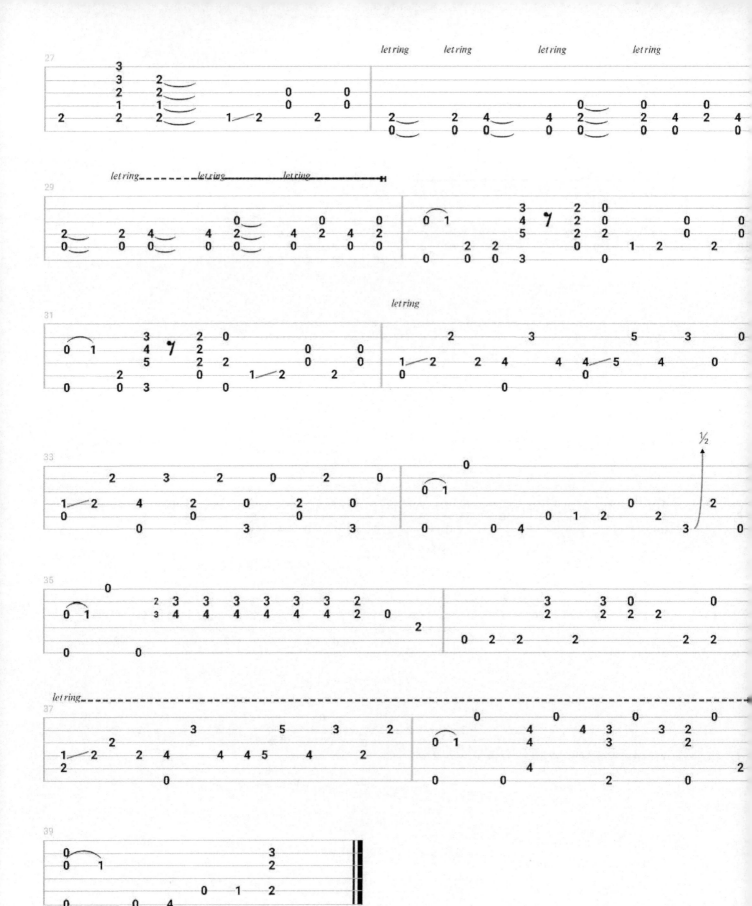

Sweet Baby James
James Taylor

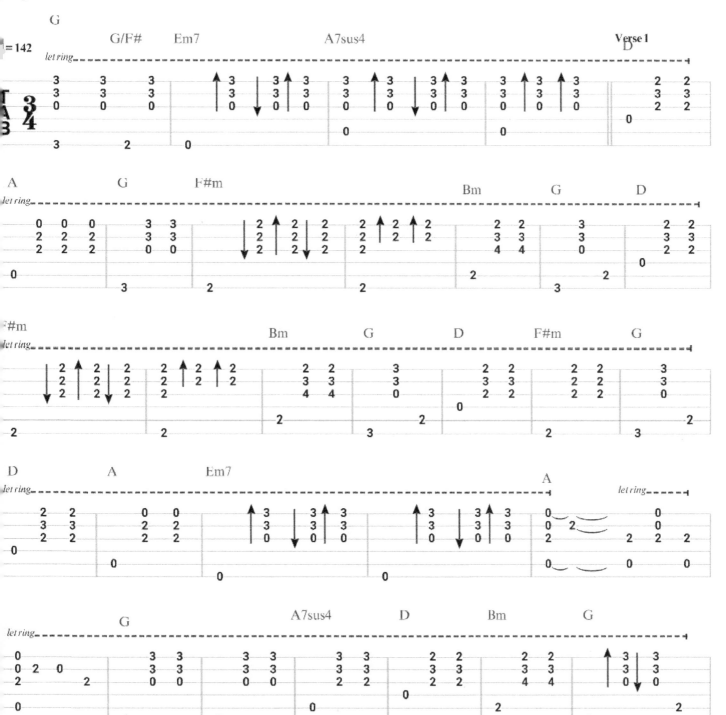

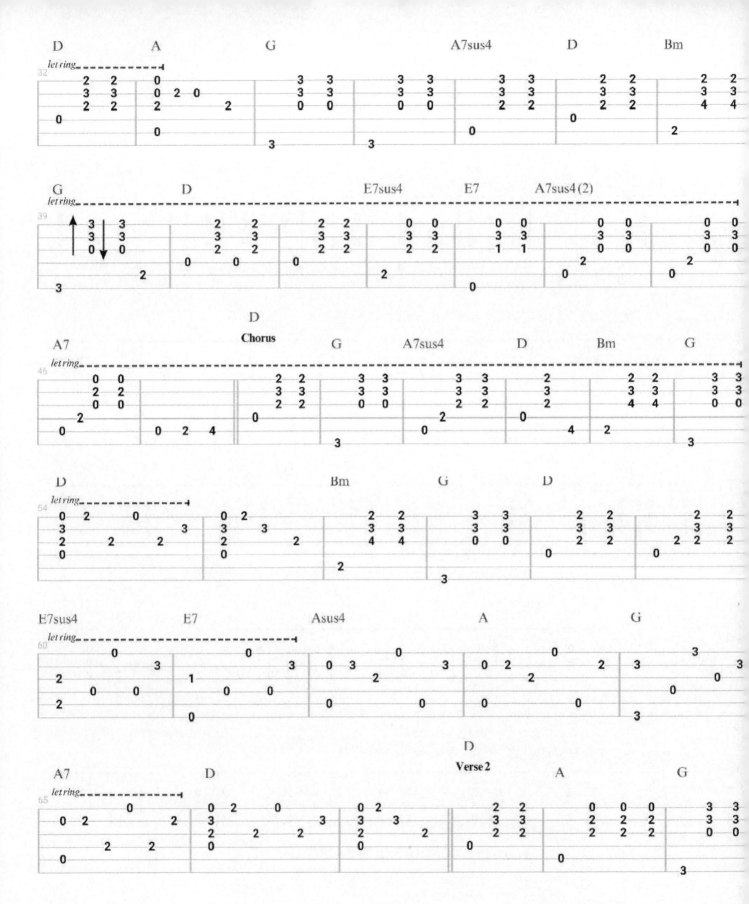

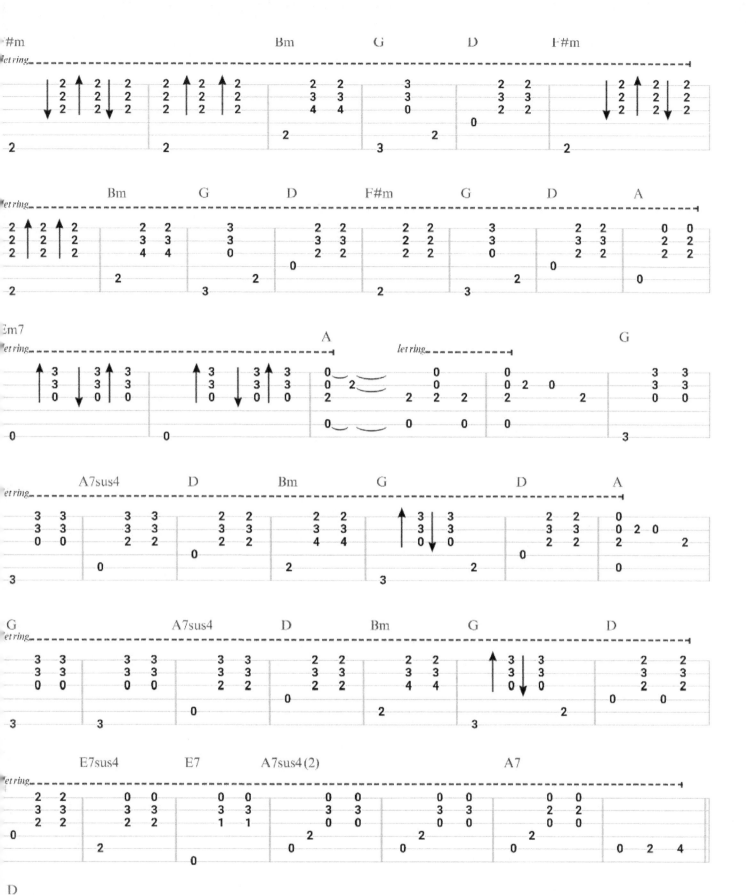

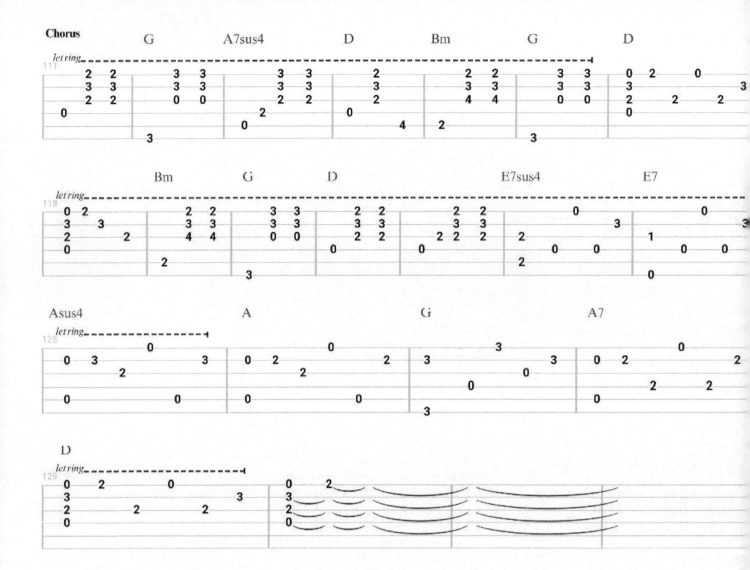

The Water Is Wide

James Taylor

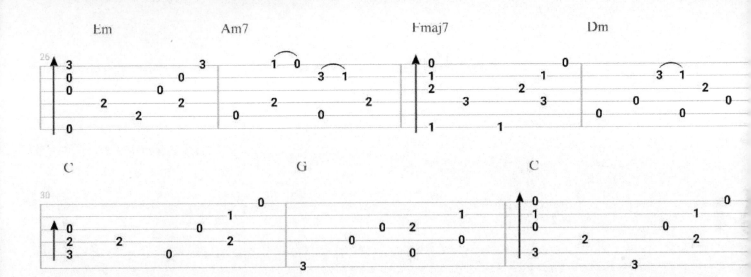

Wandering
James Taylor

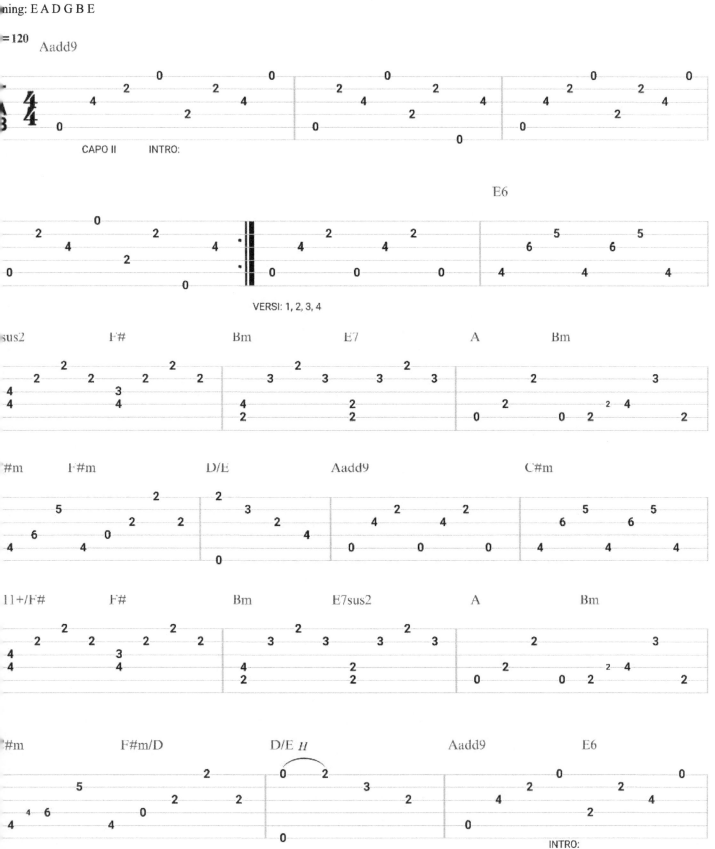

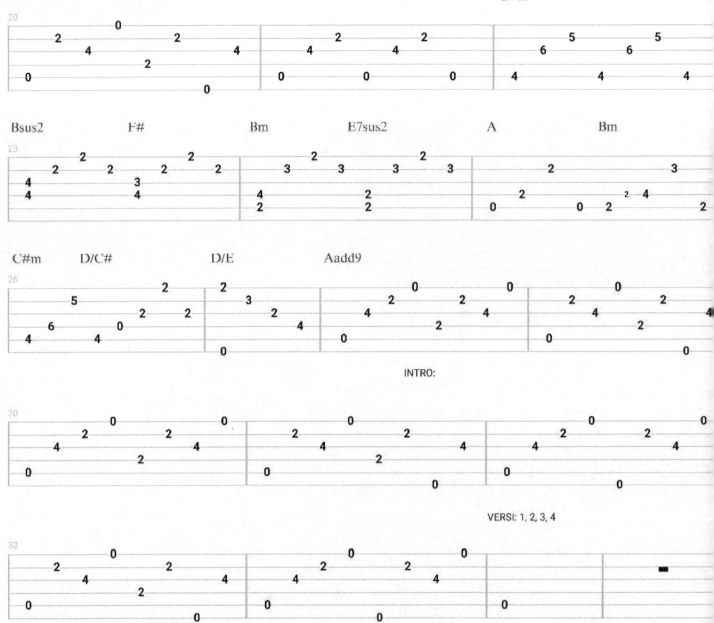

You Can Close Your Eyes

James Taylor

ning: E A D G B E

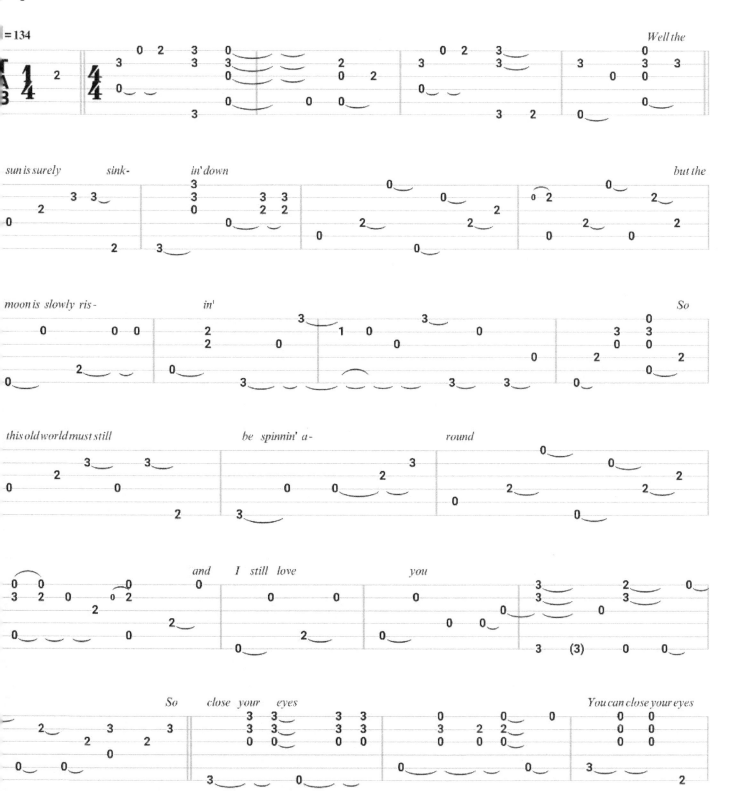

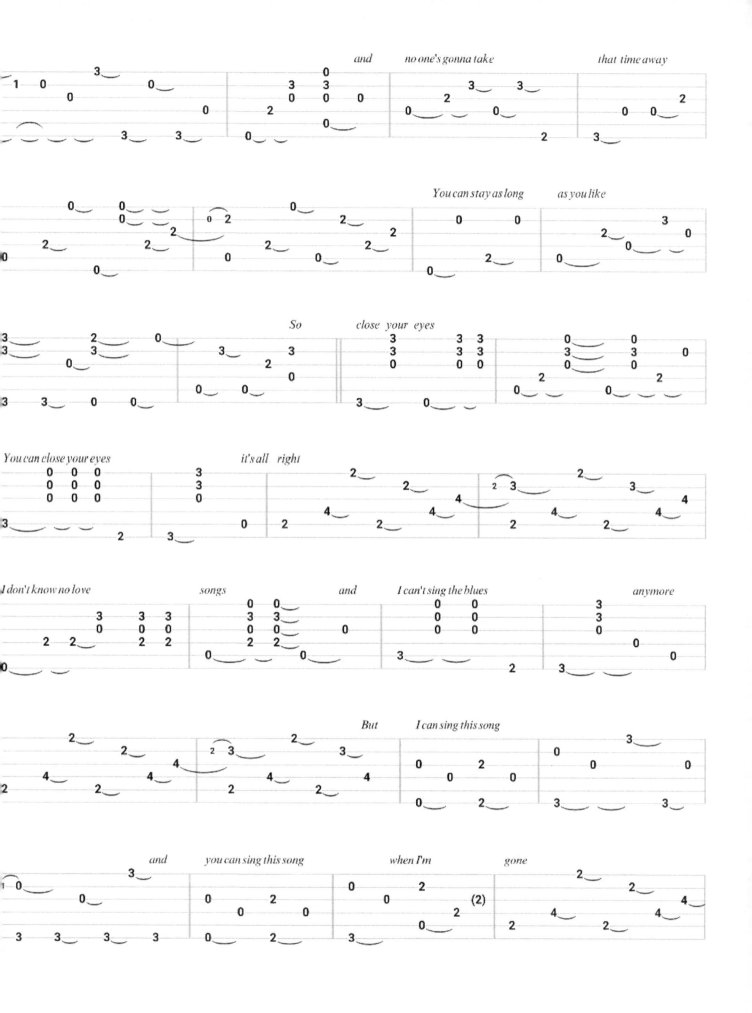

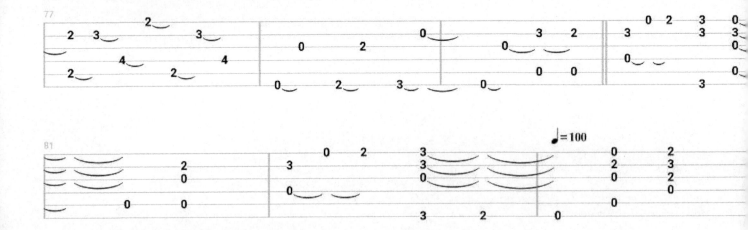

Youve Got A Friend

James Taylor

Tuning: E A D G B E

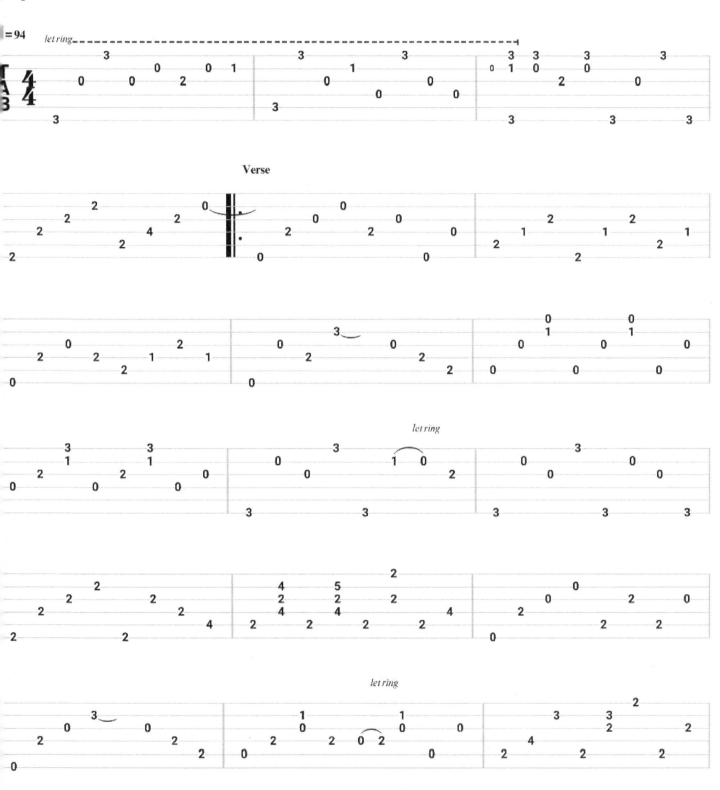

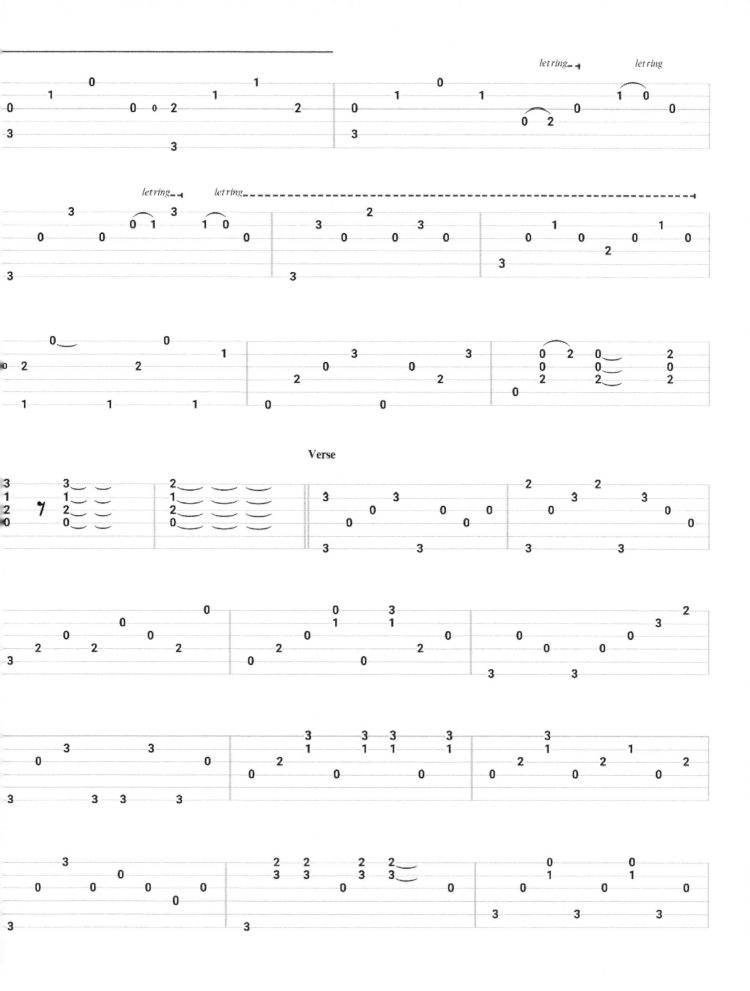

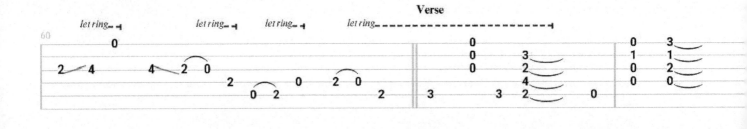
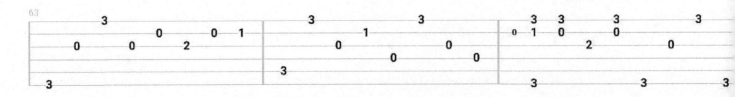

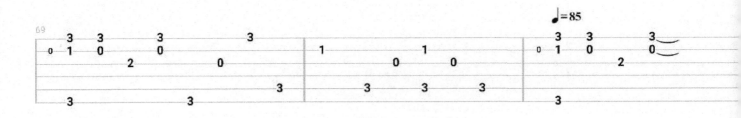

Printed in Great Britain
by Amazon

40120589R00044